They Received The Crown of Martyrdom
Dr. Robert L. La May[1]

**Let King Jesus reign,
and all His enemies be scattered.**
James Renwick

The kingdoms of this world are become
the kingdoms of our Lord and His Christ,
and He shall reign forever and ever!
Revelation 11:15

---

[1] Robert L. La May is a retired pastor of the Reformed Presbyterian Church of North America. He writes the weekly Bible Studies for the Christian Observer, Manassas, Virginia (www.christianobserver.org), and is an Associate Evangelist and Conference speaker with the Presbyterian Evangelistic Fellowship, Decatur, Georgia. He is a graduate of Tarkio College, Tarkio, Missouri, Biblical (New York Theological) Seminary, N.Y.C., and has received a Litt.D. from Covenanter College. Fort Worth, Texas. Robert and his wife, Kay live at 432 E. Van Buren St., Washington, IA 52353. Their ministry centers in the study of the Westminster Confession and its Catechism & Bible Study. Email: lamay@rpchurch.org — Web Site: www.kinder-kreations.com

[2] The Edinburgh Castle. The pictures in this book are from <u>Men Scots Worthies</u> by John Howie, and <u>The Lades of the Covenant</u> by James Anderson, unless otherwise stated.

Published by Full Bible Publications
Clover, SC 29710
3rd Edition September 2006

Full Bible Publications is an imprint of
The Christian Observer Foundation
9400 Fairview Avenue
Manassas, VA 20110

Dedicated to
> **The faithful Ministers of the Word;**
> **The faithful men and women of the Covenant;**
> **Those who faithfully preach, in one way or another,**
> **The Majesty of God, the Loveliness of Christ,**
> **And the Hope of the Gospel**
> > **to those who are sorrow of heart.**

With special thanks to Mrs. Howard (Patti) Rowe
of Muscatine for her many hours of dedicated service
in editing and proofreading to make this work possible.

---

[1] Wetherbow Port.

The writer has been encouraged with the comments of those who have read previous editions of this book. They have found it to be most profitable when these short stories are read aloud in family fellowships, at church, or even while riding in a car. The stories come alive and have more impact when read aloud this way.

Table of Contents
Contents   **Page**

Introduction
His Saints are Precious!

Scripture teaches us how excellent or costly, how **"Precious in the sight of the Lord is the death of His saints"** [Ps. 116:15[1]]. Christ Jesus speaks of those who are His that "they shall walk[2] with me in white; for they are worthy. He that overcometh, shall be clothed in white array, and I will not put out his name from the Book of Life, but I will confess his name before my Father, and before his angels" [Rev. 3:4-5]. Most precious are His saints, the sheep of His pasture, which He would desire that they would fellowship with Him.

David knew the power of God's deliverance from death to life. He understood the grace of God through His faith in his Savior and King. David loved the Lord because He inclined His heart to his: "When the snares of death compassed me, and the griefs of the grave caught me; when I found trouble and sorrow. Then I called upon the Name of the Lord, saying, I beseech thee, O Lord, deliver my soul." [Ps. 116:3-4 (GB)] David's assurance of deliverance came from his faith that his Savior was full of grace and love: "The Lord is merciful and righteous, and our God is full of compassion. The Lord preserveth the simple; I was in misery, and he saved me." [Ps. 116:5-6 (GB)]. David also knew what his position was before the Lord, "I am Thy servant and the son of Thine handmaid; Thou hast loosed my bonds" [Psalm 116:16]. There is no other name under heaven whereby the servants of the Lord are saved. Though the Christian may face bodily death, he claims the victory as Christ's faithful disciple: "O death, where is thy sting? O grave, where is thy victory? The sting of death is sin, and the strength of sin is the law. But thanks be to God who giveth us the victory through our Lord Jesus Christ!" [1 Cor. 15:55-57].

Therefore, "Precious in the sight of the Lord is the death of His saints." How precious is the blood of His saints, for whom Christ has died and set free from the wages of sin. "Albeit the Lord's children are very precious in his eyes, yet he puts them to sufferings and hazard of life, but lets them not be killed, except he sees it for his own honour and theirs also; and in that case, howsoever the world shall esteem their death, yet shall it be dear and precious in God's eyes: *precious in the eyes of the Lord is the death of his saints*" [David Dickson[3]].

---

[1] Use of KJV/Authorized Version, Geneva Bible (GB).

[2] 'Walk'—to be eternally in the presence of the Lord. "Therefore we are buried with him by baptism into death; that like Christ was raised from the dead by the glory of the Father, even so we also should walk in newness of life" (Rom. 6:4).

[3] David Dickson, The Psalms, The Banner of Truth Trust, Edinburgh, 1995, 2nd Vol. page 328.

8

Stephen

God's saints are to commit the keeping of their souls to their faithful Creator. Those whom we call *Martyrs* are our example of such a child of God. Stephen is one of the first Christians or New Testament Martyrs. As the Word of God increases the number of disciples multiplies [Acts 6:7]. Stephen was found to be "full of faith" [Acts 6:8]. Those who heard him preach were not able to resist "the Spirit by which he spoke" [Acts 6:10]. However, many were ready and willing to stir up people with lies, and setting up false witnesses against him [Acts 6:11-14]. Stephen's defense was the Word, the Gospel of the Glory of God [Acts 7:1-53]. With all their gnashing of their teeth they could not turn Stephen from his Lord. For he was filled with the Holy Spirit, and as he looked to heaven he "saw the glory of God, and Jesus standing at the right hand of God" [Acts 7:55-56]. As they stoned Stephen he called upon God, saying, "Lord Jesus, receive my spirit"[1] [Acts 7:59]. Stephen, as well as the true Martyrs of Christ (and thus of every child of the King), looks toward Christ as their *Sovereign and Saviour*, the only name under heaven who can receive their souls at the time of death, at which time they will hear Him say, "Today you will be with me in paradise!"

Two Margarets

Two of God's blessed saints that were not included in the original series in the Observer are the two Margarets. These two women were

Drowning of Margaret M'Lachlan and Margaret Wilson.

faithful to their Savior, unto death, reminding us that we too need to stand fast in our faith against a world that wars against Christ. Margaret, eighteen years old, and Agnes, thirteen, stood before a brutal court at Wigtown on April 13, 1685. They were accused of rebellion and attending both field meetings and indoor meetings for worship, along with two other ladies of the Covenant, Margaret MacLachlan,

---

[1] "The petition is not that he would take away his life or suffer him to die, as in the case of Elijah (1 Kings 19, 4) and of Jonah (4, 3), but that he would receive his soul when separated from his body. This prayer of Stephen is not only a direct imitation of our Lord's upon the cross (Luke 23, 46), but a further proof that he addressed him as a divine person, since he here asks of the Son precisely what the Son there asks of the Father" (J. A. Alexander, The Acts of the Apostles, The Banner of Truth Trust, Edinburgh, 1984, page 312.

widow of seventy years, and Margaret Maxwel, twenty years old, was a serving-maid. Margaret and Agnes were the daughters of a farmer, Gilbert Wilson. The sentences were pronounced upon the women. Agnes's father was to pay a 100-pound bond for her, but his plea for Margaret did not help. Margaret Wilson and Margaret MacLachlan were sentenced to die by drowning, and the other Margaret was to be publicly flogged through the streets of Wigtown for three days.

Margaret and her aged friend were tied to the stakes, planted within the sea's flood mark. The older Margaret was placed a little further out and so was to suffer first. The younger Margaret was asked what she thought of her friend now. She answered, "What do I see but Christ in one of his members there? Think you that we are the sufferers? No; it is Christ in us, for he sends none a warfare upon their own charges." The waters surrounded Margaret Wilson as she began to sing a song she knew from "the fellowship of the hunted worshipers." It was from the seventh verse of Psalm 25:

> My sins and faults of youth
> Do Thou O Lord forget:
> After Thy mercy think on me,
> And for Thy goodness great.
> God good and upright is:
> The way he'll sinners show;
> The meek in judgment He will guide
> And make His path to know."

The Suffering Servant knows how precious are His saints, those who suffer for His sake: "For inasmuch then as Christ has suffered for us in the flesh, arm yourselves likewise with the same mind, for he that hath suffered in the flesh hath ceased from sin, that he no longer should live the rest of his time in the flesh to the lusts of men, but to the will of God. . . . Therefore let those who suffer according to the will of God commit the keeping of their souls to Him in well doing, as unto a faithful Creator. . . . But after ye have suffered for a while, may the God of all grace, who hath called us into His eternal glory by Christ Jesus, make you perfect, establish, strengthen, and settle you. To Him be the glory and dominion for ever and ever. Amen" [1 Peter 4:1-2, 19, 5:10-11].

We should first give ourselves to the Lord that we may give ourselves to His gospel. Paul wrote of the church of Macedonia, "How that in a great trial of affliction the abundance of their joy and their deep poverty abounded unto the riches of their liberality. For to their power, I bear record, yea, and beyond their power they were willing of themselves; praying us with much entreaty that we would receive the gift, and take upon us the fellowship of the ministering to the saints. And this they did, not as we hoped, but first gave their own selves to the Lord, and unto us by the will of God" [2 Cor. 8:2-5].

The Crown of Martyrdom

Many of the stories of the men and women included in this book are those which were prepared for the Christian Observer.[1] Many of these saints faced the enemy of Christ the King during the "killing-time" or "the persecuting period"; so called because of the vast number of murders by the dragoons (horse-soldiers) in the fields. Those who were suspected of being "of a religious character," were killed without trial or warning. "The south and west of Scotland was converted into a spacious burning-field, on the wide arena of which the blood of God's saints were made to run like water. The cavaliers of those days engaged with heart and hand in the ungodly crusade against their country's liberties, and were guilty of acts of cruelty, at the bare recital of which we feel a cold shuddering creep over our frame. The heart bleeds painfully when we think on the hardships to which our virtuous ancestors were subjected, in following what they conceived to be the plain line of their duty, and in maintaining their privileges as Christians, and their rights as citizens. They dare not, as the poet says,—

'They dared not, in the face of day,
To worship God, nor even at the dead of night,
Save when the wintry storm raved fierce,
And thunder-peals compelled the men of blood
To couch within their dens; then dauntlessly
The scattered few would meet in some deep dell,
By rocks o'er-canopied, to hear the voice,
Their faithful pastor's voice, who, by the glare
Of sheeted lightning, opened the sacred book,
And words of comfort spoke.'"[2]

A personal note:

At the age of four my parents joined the Westminster United Presbyterian Church (of North America) in Brooklyn, New York. At the age of thirteen (1943) I was confirmed in my faith in Jesus Christ after being taught for two years the Question and Answers of the Westminster Shorter Catechism. There were eight of us in the class, two boys and six

[1] The Christian Observer, 9400 Fairview Avenue, Manassas, Va. 20110-5802.
[2] Rev. Robert Simpson, Traditions of the Covenanters, Presbyterian Board of Education. Philadelphia, pages 5-6.

girls (I have the group picture on my wall). The preaching was of the Word and the fellowship was good.

The United Presbyterian Church was still faithfully teaching the Westminster Confession and its Catechisms at this time. I had, therefore, a fair foundation as I entered the ministry, being ordained in 1963. The battle was waging and we were moving further away from the truth of the Bible and, therefore, from a Confessional stand.

I still have a love for the 'Old' United Presbyterian fellowship, though I left the body in 1973. A number of years ago I came across a book written by a group of ministers in the United Presbyterian Church during the battle over Psalmody and Hymnody. I have include two full chapters from this book (The Psalms in Worship, 1907) because of its stand for the exclusive singing of God's song Book, i.e., the Psalms; thus their stand on the Word of God. The two chosen papers are from two presidents of colleges I am familiar with: One written by President Spencer of Sterling College, Kansas; the other by President Thompson of Tarkio College, Missouri. Both of these men refer to the time of the Martyrs. These papers, as well as the short tales of the Martyrs, should remind us that it is the Word of God and of the Christ, the Prince and Head of the Church, which brings about faithfulness in His servants, and persecution from His enemies.

Those who have gone on before us must know that the banner has been passed on, that it is held high, unashamedly displayed as the Banner of Faith and Grace, to the glory of Christ our King! They carried the Banner to the preaching fields when they could not preach in the churches. They catechized the families in the precious Word of God. They penetrated the courts of the kings, for they had a great love for their Savior, His Church, and the Nation. "Let King Jesus reign, and all His enemies be scattered" [James Renwick].

Robert L. La May

"Beloved, think it not strange concerning the fiery trial which is to try you, as though some strange thing happened unto you' but rejoice inasmuch as ye are partakers of Christ's sufferings; that, when his glory shall be revealed, ye may be glad also with exceeding joy. If ye be reproached for the name of Christ, happy are ye; for the spirit of glory and of God resteth upon you; on their part he is evil spoken of, but on your part he is glorified."

I Peter 4:12-14

Song from God's Word
I Love the Lord
Psalm 116A [tune: OSTEND. C.M.D.][1]

I love the LORD because He heard My supplicating plea;
I while I live will call on Him Who bowed His ear to me.
The cords of death on every side Encompassed me around;
The sorrows of the grave took hold; I grief and trouble found.
Then called I on Jehovah's name And unto Him did say,
"Deliver Thou my soul, O LORD, I do Thee humbly pray."
The LORD is gracious and is just; Our God will mercy show;
The LORD preserves the meek in heart; He saved me when brought low.
O thou my soul, do thou return To thine own quiet rest,
Because the LORD has dealt in grace; His bounty has thee blessed.
Thou hast release my soul from death, My eyes from tears kept free;
From falling Thou has saved my feet; I live and walk with THEE.

Psalm 116B [tune: SOUL'S SURRENDER. C.M]
I still believed, although I said, "How sorely I am tried!"
Though I asserted in my haste, "All living men have lied."
What shall I render to the LORD? What shall my off'ring be
For all the gracious benefits He has bestowed on me?
I'll lift salvation's cup, O LORD, And on Jehovah call;
I'll pay my vows now to the LORD Before His people all.
The death of all His saints the LORD Is deeply moved to see.
O LORD, I am Thy handmaid's son, Thy slave, by Thee set free.
To Thee thankofferings I'll bring And on Jehovah call.
I'll pay my vows now to the LORD Before His people all,
Within His courts, Jehovah's house, Yes, in the midst of thee,
O city of Jerusalem. Praise to the LORD give ye.

---

[1] The Book of Psalms for Singing, Crown and Covenant Pub., Pittsburgh, Pa.

The Song of the Saints

There is a song to be sung by each of God's saints. It is a song of salvation, testifying before Christ, "Thou are worthy to take the book and to open the seals thereof; for Thou wast slain, and hast redeemed us to God by Thy blood, from every kindred and tongue, and people and nation, and hast made us unto our God kings and priests; and we shall reign on earth." There is the song for ten thousand times ten thousands, saying with a loud voice, "Worthy is the Lamb that was slain, to receive power and riches and wisdom and strength, and honor and glory and blessing!" [Rev. 5:9-12]

The character of the persecutors and of the persecuted is seen in these stories. Scripture testifies of the wicked and the righteous: "But, beloved, remember ye the words which were spoken before of the apostle of our Lord Jesus Christ; how that they told you there shall be mockers in the last time, who should walk after their own ungodly lusts. These be they who separate themselves, sensual, having not the Spirit. But ye, beloved, building up yourselves on your most holy faith, praying in the Holy Spirit, keep yourselves in the love of God, looking for the mercy of our Lord Jesus Christ unto eternal life" [Jude 1:17-21]. The followers of the evil one rebel against their Creator. The Christian must be reminded of the fight he must face. Or else God's Scripture has no meaning for us. For we are told, "Finally, my brethren, be strong in the Lord and in the power of His might. Put on the whole armor of God, that ye may be able to stand against the wiles of the devil" [Eph. 6:10-11].

"What tragic tears bedim the eye!
What deaths we suffer ere we die"

Dr. W. H. Carslaw wrote of the Covenanter Martyrs, speaking of them as "Exiles of the Covenant."[1] He introduces chapter one with the following definition of a martyr:

"The word 'martyr' has a much wider meaning and application than is generally recognized in popular speech. It is a Greek word which signifies a witness or witness-bearer, and is frequently employed in the New Testament to describe one who has seen or heard something, and is willing to testify to its truth. By and by, however, it came to be applied only to those who sealed their testimony with their blood; and when we speak of our Scottish martyrs it is generally in this narrower and more restricted sense the word is understood. Of these, the number was by no

---

[1] W. H. Carslaw, D.D., Exiles of the Covenant, Paisley Alexander Gardner, Publisher by Appointment to the late Queen Victoria, 1908.

means inconsiderable during the first Reformation; while during the twenty-eight miserable years between the Restoration and the Revolution, apart from untold hardships and sufferings, the slain on the scaffold and in the fields cannot have fallen much short of two thousand. Even on the testimony of so sane a writer as the author of the *Men of the Covenant*, 'those killed in skirmish and insurrection were at least 680'; 'in the fields and on the hillsides 500 were slain in cold blood'; 'while 360 were executed after some form of examination had been perfunctorily and summarily hurried through.' Moreover, as he truly adds, 'it is impossible to count the men and women and children who succumbed to rain and frost and fatigue and hunger in their wanderings across mosses and mountains.' In this connection it is important to remember how small Scotland is compared with other countries, and how thinly populated it was at that time. At the end of the fifteenth century it is believed that the population did not exceed half a million, Edinburgh having about 20,000, followed by Perth with about 9,000, Glasgow 5,000 or 6,000, and Aberdeen, Dundee, and St. Andrews each with about 4,000. By the time of the Union in 1707, it is believed to have reached a million, while at the time of the first Government census in 1801 the total number was 1,608,420. That, out of a population of certainly less than a million, so many should have been willing to sacrifice their lives in defense of civil and religious liberty, is one of the noblest testimonies to the power of conscience, and to the all sufficiency of God's grace.

"To form an accurate or even approximate idea of the sufferings of our fathers, we must, however, take into account, among other things, the bitterness of banishment which many had to taste, and to which Dante refers in the immortal lines—

> 'Thou shalt leave each thing
> Beloved most dearly: this is the first shaft
> Shot from the bow of exile. Thou shalt prove
> How salt the savour is of others' bread,
> How hard the passage to descend and climb
> By others' stairs. But that shall gall thee most
> Will be the worthless and vile company
> With whom must be thrown into these straits.'"

We would be amiss if we did not understand that it was the strength of Calvinism that led the parade of Martyrs. For Calvinism sets Christ the Sovereign King and His word as their Banner. "The Reformation in Scotland," writes Boettner, "resulted in the establishment of a Calvinistic Presbyterianism in which Christ alone was recognized as the head of the

Church."[1] Boettner came to the conclusion that "the very clear testimony of history (is) that Calvinism has been the creed of saints and Heroes. 'Whatever the cause,' says Froude, 'the Calvinists were the only fighting Protestants. It was they whose faith gave them courage to stand up for the Reformation, and but for them the Reformation would have been lost.' During those centuries in which spiritual tyranny was numbering its victims by the thousands; when in England, Scotland, Holland and Switzerland, Protestantism had to maintain itself with the sword, Calvinism proved itself the only system able to cope with and destroy the great powers of the Romish Church. Its unequalled array of martyrs is one of its crowns of glory."[2]

Christ the King

How doth Christ execute the office of a king?[3]

Christ executeth the office of a king, in calling out of the world a people to himself, and giving them officers, laws, and censures by which he visibly governs them; in bestowing saving grace upon his elect, rewarding their obedience, and correcting them for their sins, preserving and supporting them under all their temptations and sufferings, restraining and overcoming all their enemies, and powerfully ordering all things for his own glory, and their good; and also in taking vengeance on the rest, who know not God, and obey not the gospel.

The King promises a crown:

"Blessed is the man that endureth temptation; for when he is tried, he shall receive the crown of life, which the Lord hath promised to them that love him."

James 1:12

---

[1] Loraine Boettner, <u>The Reformed Doctrine of Predestination</u>, The Presbyterian and Reformed Publishing Co., Phillipsburgh, N.J., 1979, page 374.

[2] Ibid, page 481.

[3] The Larger Catechism Q&A 45; <u>Westminster Confession of Faith</u>, Free Presbyterian Publications, Glasgow, 2001, pages 1490150.

The Servant in Battle[1]

O Lord,
I bless thee that the issue of the battle between thyself and Satan
   has never been uncertain,
   and will end in victory.
Calvary broke the dragon's head,
   and I contend with a vanquished foe,
   who with all his subtlety and strength
   has already been overcome.
When I feel the serpent at my heel
   may I remember him whose heel was bruised,
   but who, when bruised, broke the devil's head.

My soul with an inward joy extols the mighty conqueror.

Heal me of any wounds received in the great conflict;
   if I have gathered defilement,
   if my faith has suffered damage,
   if my hope is less than bright,
   if my love is not fervent,
   if some creature-comfort occupies my heart,
   if my soul sinks under pressure of the fight.
O thou whose every promise is balm,
   every touch life,
   draw near to thy weary warrior,
   refresh me, that I may rise again to wage the strife,
   and never tire until my enemy is trodden down.
Give me such fellowship with thee that I may defy Satan,
   unbelief, the flesh, the world,
   with delight that comes not from a creature,
   and which a creature cannot mar.
Give me a draught of the eternal fountain
   that lieth in thy immutable, everlasting love and decree.
Then shall my hand never weaken, my feet never stumble,
   my sword never rest, my shield never rust,
   my helmet never shatter, my breastplate never fall,
    as my strength rests in the power of thy might.

---

[1] The Valley of Vision, Arthur Bennett, ed., The Banner of Truth Trust, Edinburgh, 1977, page 181.

Archibald Campbell, Marquis of Argyle
He received the crown of martyrdom

Richard Campbell received a good classical education, and afterward applied himself to the study of Holy Scripture. He stood firm in the Presbyterian and Puritan faith. When Samuel Rutherford was brought before the High Commission Court in 1638, Campbell interceded on his behalf. Rutherford wrote of him, "My Lord has brought me a friend from the Highlands of Argyle . . . who hath done as much as was within the compass of his power. God gave me favour in his eyes." Lady Kenmuir wrote, "Write thanks to your brother . . . for what he has done for me, a poor unknown stranger to him. I shall pray for him and his house where I live. It is his honour to open his mouth in the streets for his wronged and oppressed Master, Christ Jesus."

In 1637 Campbell began to espouse the cause of the Reformation in Scotland. In the next year, Campbell, the Earl of Argyle (his father having died), attended the famous General Assembly held at Glasgow, agreeing with their decisions. He began to distinguish himself as one who sought his Redeemer's glory, and was faithful until he received the crown of martyrdom.

When King Charles I disagreed with his English Parliament, touring Scotland and attending the Scots Parliament, the Earl of Argyle found favor in his eyes. The King appointed him as head of the treasury. He then created Archibald Earl of Argyle, Marquis of Argyle, Earl of Kinlyre, Lord Lorne, etc. However, some of the Nobility, envying the new power and influence of the Marquis of Argyle, plotted to destroy him. The Marquis continued to have an active hand in carrying on the work of the Reformation, among the Covenanters in particular. He also used his influence to bring home Charles II. The King was crowned at Scone, January 1, 1651, the Marquis of Argyle setting the crown on the head of the King.

The King soon turned against Archibald. He called the Marquis into his presence, where he ordered him carried to the Tower. In February of 1661 his lordship was brought down from the Castle. Before the bar of the House of Parliament, Sir John Fletcher, the King's advocate, accused him of high treason. After the indictment was read, he was allowed to speak. He confessed that by solemn oath and covenant he served his God, his king, and his country. Over the months depositions were heard against him. The Marquis was found guilty of treason and "adjudged to be executed to death as a traitor, his head to be severed from his body at the Cross of Edinburgh." On a Monday in 1661 he faced his death with these words, "I had the honour to set the crown on the King's head, and now he hastens me to a better crown than his own."

Archibald kneeled down and prayed. He then raised his hand; and the instrument, called the Maiden, struck off his head from his body, which was then fixed on the west end of the Tollbooth. His body was carried to Dunoon and buried in Kilmun church.

The noble Marquis of Argyle, the proto-martyr to religion, was the head of the Covenanters in Scotland. He stuck close to the work of the Reformation, when most of the nation had abandoned it. It was written that "he had a piety for a Christian, sense for a counselor, courage for a martyr, and soul for a king. If any was, he might be said to be a true Scotsman."

The Crown of Martyrdom is a Crown of Life

"Fear none of those things which thou shalt suffer; behold, the devil shall cast some of you into prison, that ye may be tried; and ye shall have tribulation ten days; be thou faithful unto death, and I will give thee a crown of life. He that hath an ear, let him hear what the Spirit saith unto the churches; he that overcometh shall not be hurt of the second death."
–Christ Jesus to Smyrna (Rev. 2:10-11)

"Ten days of tribulation in exchange for one thousand years of victory (Rev. 20:4-6). Even so, the time of testing was to cost the lives of many in the church, and they are exhorted to be faithful until death, in order to wind the crown of life. This is not a blessing reserved for some unusually consecrated class of Christians, for all Christians are to be faithful until death. The Bible simply does not know of any other kind of Christian. 'If we endure, we shall also reign with Him; if we deny Him, He also will deny us" (2 Tim. 2:12). 'Your will be hated by all on account of My name,' Jesus said; 'but it is the one who has endured to the end who will be saved' (Matt. 10:22). The crown of life is salvation itself."
–David Chilton[1]

---

[1] David Chilton, The Days Of Vengeance, ibid, page 104.

Samuel Rutherford
"I shall see Him reign"

Charles II came to the throne in 1660, threatening to do harm to the Church of Scotland. A Scottish Parliament met on New Years day of 1661. During the Session of 1661, Parliament passed no less than 393 Acts. The Earl of Middleton, the Commissioner of King Charles, stands foremost in the affairs of Parliament. He was a man without human compassion or faith. The first session set its course of action. Its grand design "was to make the King absolute." The framers of the laws had their work cut out for them; to "demolish the outworks and bulwarks of the Church . . ." The nickname given to this House was the "Drunken Parliament." In this darkness stands one of Christ's chosen representatives, Samuel Rutherford.

Four of the leaders of the Covenant were marked for execution by Parliament. They were, Samuel Rutherford, the Marquis of Argyle, James Guthrie and Archibald Johnston. Only Samuel Rutherford escaped the martyr's death. Samuel Rutherford rested his faith firmly on his Savior: "I never knew before, that His love was in such a measure. If He leave me, He leaves me in pain, and sick of life; and yet my sickness is my life and health. I have fire within me; I defy all the devils in hell, and all the prelates in Scotland, to cast water upon it."

Samuel Rutherford was born in the year 1600, in the parish of Nisbet, in Roxburghshire. He entered the University in Edinburgh in 1617, where he received a Master of Arts. He was elected as one of the Regents of the college. After two years he left this charge and devoted himself to the study of Theology under Mr. Andrew Ramsay. In 1627 he was licensed to preach the Gospel, appointed to a church in the parish of Anwoth, Kirkcudbright. During this time the Church of Scotland felt the heavy hand of the Episcopal Bishops. The Presbyterians were cruelly oppressed because of their refusal to conform to their discipline, holding firmly onto the Presbyterian form of government. Rutherford adhered firmly to the Presbyterian form of government since his the time of his youth. It is said that Rutherford entered the ministry before the door was being closed to honest preachers. It was his custom to rise early in the morning, devoting his time to the spiritual needs of his congregation, and those of his own spiritual needs.

Five years after their marriage, in 1630, Rutherford's wife died after a painful illness of thirteen months. This brought much sorrow to his heart, and it was a long while before he was able to perform his ministerial duties. He would soon again minister to the souls of God's people. He had a heart for Scotland that the people of that land would find victory and solace in Him. He preached, "Scotland will have a new growth, like a second growth, that grows after a long hot drought. There will be many sweet calm showers, which will make our withered garden grow green again; and so become a fair green garden with many pleasant flowers. Seek to be among Christ's little ones, and covenant yourself away to Him, that so ye may be able to say, the Lord is your God; and that He may acknowledge you to be His people. And, if you are His, there is no fear of a happy out-gate, though you should have ever so many straits, trials, and difficulties in the way. The Lord enable you to close with Him. Amen."[1]

Samuel Rutherford was one of the Scots commissioners appointed in 1643 to the Westminster Assembly. He was loved for his "unparalleled faithfulness and zeal in going about his Master's business." It was at this time that he published "Lex Rex." The Law is King! He showed that all authority, even that of the king is derived from God alone; i.e., "God is the author of civil laws and government, and his intention is therein the external peace, and quiet life, and godliness of his church and people, and that all judges, according to their places, be nurse-fathers to the church. (Isa. xlix. 23.)"[2]

After the death of Cromwell in 1658, Charles II was restored to the throne. "The Scottish Parliament met in 1651, when the national covenant was recalled–and all the decrees of Parliament, since 1638, which sanctioned the Presbyterian system, were rescinded. The rights of the people were thus torn from them – their liberties trampled upon – and the whole period which followed, till the martyrdom of Renwick in 1688, was a scene of intolerant persecution and bloodshed. Rutherford, as may be supposed, did not escape persecution in such a state of things. His work, Lex Rex, was considered by the government as 'inveighing against monarchie and laying ground for rebellion;'"[3] King Charles had it burned at the cross of Edinburgh where many martyrs had stepped into their Savior's heaven. In the year 1651, when Rutherford was the professor of divinity, an indictment was brought against him at the gates of St. Andrews. However, the King of kings called Rutherford to a higher court. He replied to the indictment by telling them, "I have got a summons already before a superior judge and judicatory, and I behoove

---

[1] Rev. Samuel Rutherford, COMMUNION SERMONS, reprinted from Glasgow, 1877, James A. Dickson, Edinburgh, 1986, page 59.
[2] Samuel Rutherford, Lex, Rex, Sprinkle Pub., Harrisonburg, Va., 1982, page 105.
[3] Ibid, "Sketch of the Life of Samuel Rutherford," page xix.

to answer my first summons, and ere your day come I will be where few kings and great folks come."

Rutherford was forever exalting his Lord Jesus, calling Him his Master, his kingly King. A few days before his death, he said, "I shall shine - I shall see Him as He is - I shall see Him reign, and all His fair company with Him; and I shall have my large share. Mine eyes shall see my Redeemer . . ." On the 20th day of March, Samuel Rutherford breathed his last words, "Glory, glory, dwelleth in Emmanuel's land."

The last line of a poem by Harriet S. Menteath, "The Deathbed of Rutherford," tells the story of the one who gave his life for his Savior and nation: "They give his writings to the flames; they brand his grave with shame; A hissing in the mouth of fools becomes his honored name; And darkness wraps awhile the land, for which he prayed and strove, But blessed in the Lord his death, and blest his rest above!"

His letters and other writings should be a must reading for every Christian, especially for Christian statesmen who wish to see their nation blessed.

The Killing Times were reddest in 1685. Daniel Defoe, author of Robinson Crusoe, was most sympathetic of the Covenanters. He wrote that the barbarities of this year supported his opinion that the Scottish persecution was worse than that of the Roman Emperors or Popish Inquisitors.

*"God is no mere spectator of the universe He has made,
but is everywhere present and active,
the all sustaining ground, and all governing power of all
that is.*

Although the price of the sparrow is small and its flight seems giddy and at random, yet it does not fall to the ground, nor alight anywhere without your Father. 'His all-wise providence hath before appointed what bough it shall perch upon; what grains it shall pick up; where it shall lodge and where it shall build; on what it shall live and where it shall die' [Toplady].

Every rain drop and every snowflake which falls from the cloud, every insect which moves, every plant which grows, every grain of dust which floats in the air has had certain definite causes and will have certain definite effects. Each is a link in the chain of events and many of the great events of history have turned on these apparently insignificant events."[1]

Of Providence[2]

God the great Creator of all things doth uphold, direct, dispose, and govern all creatures, actions and things, from the greatest to the least, by His most wise and holy providence, according to His infallible foreknowledge, and the free and immutable counsel of His own will, to the praise of the glory of His wisdom, power, justice, goodness, and mercy.

---

[1] Loraine Boettner, The Reformed Doctrine of Predestination, The Presbyterian and Reformed Publishing Co., Phillipsburg, NJ, 1979, page 37.

[2] Westminster Confession of Faith, ibid, Of Providence, pages 33-34. Christ "Who being the brightness of his glory, and the express image of his person, and upholding all things by the word of his power, when he had by himself purged our sins, sat down on the right hand of the Majesty on high" [Hebrews 1:3].

Robert Baillie
Distinguished for his Learning

Robert Baillie was born at Glasgow on April 30, 1602. His father was of the lineage of Baillie of Jerviston; his mother of the Gibsons of Durie. His first wife was Lilias Fleming. They had one son and four daughters. His second wife was the daughter of Principal Strang. They had one daughter.

He received his education at Glasgow and proved himself as a scholar learning some twelve languages. His studies included that of theology, taking orders from Archbishop Law in 1622. The time of the Reformation brought about his decision to join with the Covenanting community. In 1638 Robert Baillie was chosen by the presbytery to be a member of the Assembly at Glasgow. He was one of the chaplains to the army in the years 1639 and 1640. He accepted the invitation to be Professor of Divinity at the University of Glasgow.

In the year 1643 he was sent as a Commissioner from the Church of Scotland to the Westminster Assembly at London, along with his colleagues Rutherford and Gillespie. Though Baillie[1] did not take a prominent part in the Assembly's deliberations, his letters gave us much information on the procedure and spirit of the Westminster Assembly. The character of the Assembly is seen in these observations of Baillie: "Every committee, as the Parliament gives orders in writing to take any purpose to consideration, takes a portion, and on the afternoon meeting, prepares matters for the Assembly, sets down its mind in distinct propositions, backing these propositions with texts of Scripture. After the prayer, Mr. Byfield, the scribe, reads the propositions with texts of Scriptures, whereupon the Assembly debates, in a most grave and orderly way. No man is called upon to speak; but whosoever stands up of his own accord speaks so long as he will without interruption. If two or three stand up at once, then the divines confusedly call on his name whom they desire to hear first. On whom the loudest and maniest voices call, he speaks. No man speaks to any, but the prolocutor. They harangue long, and very learnedly. They study the question well beforehand, and prepare their speeches. But withal, the men are exceedingly prompt and well spoken. I do marvel at the very accurate and extemporal replies hat many of them usually make."[2]

---

[1] "Baillie's letters give us the most extensive, if not the most minute, accounts, embracing as they do the whole period, and are written in that peculiar, quaint, graphic style for which the author is distinguished, and which never fails to interest and delight the reader." –Wm Symington, Historical Sketch of the Westminster Divines, page 3.

[2] John Howie, The Scots Worthies, Edinburgh and London, page 283.

Robert Baillie returned home, along with the some of the Scottish Commissioners, after a year in London to give a progress report on the Assembly. Traveling by horseback they left on the sixth of January 1645, arriving at Newcastle on the eighteenth. They arrived in Edinburgh and reported to the General Assembly. Baillie visited his family at Glasgow, returning to London before the end of March, where he spent two years at the Assembly; returning again to present to a meeting of the Commission in January of 1647. He presented the Confession of Faith and the new metrical version of the Psalms. He gave this account of the labours of the divines: "It is one of Lord's promises to us, that they who sow in tears shall reap in joy; that they who go out weeping, and carry precious seed, shall return with rejoicing, and bring their sheaves. It was the General Assembly's pleasure, some four years ago, to send some of us, their weak brethren and servants, to that venerable and worthy Synod at Westminster, to sow, in that famous place, some of the precious seed, not of our Church, as enemies do slander, but of God, the Father of all light and truth."[1]

The Lords and Commons, having assembled in Parliament, called an Assembly of learned and godly Divines, for the purpose of vindicating and clearing of the doctrine of the Church from false aspersions and interpretations. The Divines assembled themselves at Westminster, in the Chapel called King Henry VII's Chapel on July 1, 1643.[2] There the teaching of Holy Scripture motivated the discussions of the liturgy, discipline, worship, and government of the Church.

HENRY VII. CHAPEL—WESTMINSTER ABBEY.

No sooner had the Reformation of the Church and nation had begun, before the spirit of the Westminster Assembly fully closed its doors, darkness began to cloud the Light that so faithfully shined through the earnest work of the divines.[3] In the year of 1650 Commissioners were sent to renew negotiations with Charles, who sailed with them to Spey. "Before Charles landed on the Scottish shore he agreed to swear and subscribe the

---

[1] Ibid, page 285.

[2] The Confession of Faith was approved by the General Assembly of Scotland in 1647; and "ratified and established by Acts of Parliament 1649 and 1690, as the Public and avowed Confession of the Church of Scotland, with proofs from the Scripture." –Westminster Confession of Faith, Free Presbyterian Publications, page 19.

[3] It should be a warning to the true Church today, that the fight we fight, the armor that we wear, the Book which builds our moral character, the Gospel which proceeds from our pulpits, must never be taken for granted. For the Church must not let its guard down. The enemy is as cunning as its benefactor, of Satan himself.

covenant. Mr. Livingstone, who accompanied the embassy, and was very jealous of the king's sincerity, would have deferred this ceremony till he was brought to a better state of mind; but he was overruled by the rest, and prevailed on reluctantly to administer the solemn test;" the Church was suspicious of Charles, and in August he did declare to renounce Popery and Prelacy, and "would have no enemies but the enemies of the covenant—no friends but the friends of the covenant."[1] His profession would soon be seen as a lie as he embraced Popery.

Kings and senators, presidents and prime ministers, leaders of nations and magistrates of counties, can seem to adhere to religious or moral beliefs while harboring their own twisted goals, faithful only to their belief that the end justifies the means. Thus Charles could easily be crowned on January of 1651, and patently listen to a sermon by Robert Douglas from 2 Kings xi, 12, 17; hearing this admonition, "Let your sincerity be evidenced by your steadfastness and constancy; for many, like your ancestor, have begun well, but have not been constant. Take warning from the example before you; let it be laid to your heart; requite not the Lord so, who preserved you at this time, and is setting a crown on your head."[2] The National Covenant and Solemn League were then read and the oath taken to support the Church of Scotland; and as he kneeled he made this promise (which he did not keep), "By the Eternal and Almighty God, who liveth and reigneth forever, I shall observe and keep all that is contained in this oath."

It was not long before king Charles broke covenant, which was but an outward show, and schism took place with the formation of two parties at the Assembly at St. Andrews in 1651; "Those who adhered to the resolutions[3] or answers given by the commission were called Resolutioners; those who joined in a protest against them were denominated Protestors."[4] Though Robert Baillie joined the Resolutioner, he would remain faithful to the Presbyterian government, apposing the Prelacy.

Robert Baillie, by the undertaking of Lauderdale, was made Principal of the College of Glasgow. Baillie had much esteem for Lauderdale, but began to understand the schism faced by church and parliament. He wrote to Lauderdale, "If you have gone with your heart to forsake your covenant, to countenance the re-introduction of bishops and books, and

---

[1] Thomas M'Crie, <u>The Story of the Scottish Church</u>, Free Presbyterian Publications, Glasgow, page 233.
[2] Ibid, page 236.
[3] I.e., Resolutions were passed that would allow 'friends' of Charles to obtain high positions in the government.
[4] Ibid, page 238.

strengthen the King by your advice in those things, I think you are a prime transgressor, and liable among the first to answer for that great sin." The Archbishop came to visit Baillie at his deathbed, and would not give him the blessing of the Lord. Baillie wrote to his cousin, Mr. Spang, May 12, 1662, "The guise is now, the bishops will trouble no man, but the states will punish seditious ministers. This poor Church is in the most hard taking that ever we have seen. This is my daily grief; this hath brought all my bodily trouble on me, and is like to do me more harm."[1] Soon after, in the month of July, Baillie got to his heavenly reward at the age of sixty-three.

The Spirit of 1650

"An English merchant, who had occasion to visit Scotland in the way of business about the year 1650, happened to hear three of the most eminent of the Scottish ministers of that age—Robert Blair, Samuel Rutherford, and David Dickson. Being asked, on his return, what news he had brought from Scotland, the gentleman, who had never shown any sense of religion before, replied, 'Great and good news! I went to St. Andrews, where I heard a sweet majestic-looking man (Blair); and he showed me the *majesty of God*. After him, I heard a little fair man (Rutherford); and he showed me *the loveliness of Christ*. I then went to Irvine, where I heard a well-favoured proper old man, with a long beard (Dickson); and that man showed me *all my heart*.'"[2]

---

[1] The Scots Worthies, ibid, page 286.
[2] The Story of the Scottish Church, ibid, page 248.

Divine History

All of history is of a 'CELESTIAL' nature. Divine in structure, true history reveals the work (which includes His providential care) of the Sovereign Creator. John Calvin wrote that the *Certainty about God's providence puts joyous trust toward God in our hearts*;[1] which gives much encouragement to those whose lives are lived to Christ unto death. Calvin continues, "Yet when the light of divine providence has once shone upon a godly man, he is then relieved and set free not only from the extreme anxiety and fear that were pressing him before, but from every care. For as he justly dreads fortune, so he fearlessly dares commit himself to God. His solace, I say, is to know that his Heavenly Father so holds all things in his power, so rules by his authority and will, so governs by his wisdom, that nothing can befall except he determine it. Moreover, it comforts him to know that he has been received in God's safekeeping and entrusted to the care of his angels, and that neither water, nor fire, nor iron can harm him, except in so far as it pleases God as governor to given them occasion."

The past as well as the future is our inheritance. "To say that there is nothing interesting in the remnants of antiquity, is to say that there is nothing interesting in the past. The feudal tower, or an old monumental stone, or a druidical circle, or a lonely cairn on the waste, serves to commemorate, form a portion of the history of our race, and God is in that history"[2]

As there is calm after the storm, there is calm before the tornado strikes. Thus the brightness of the Reformation unchained the Bible from the dungeons of Rome, followed by persecution. The Reformation brought about by the Westminster Assembly was also followed by persecution. Faithfulness to Christ the King and His glorious written Word find the breath of life to face the storms of deception and persecution. Though this book hinges on the persecution of the Scottish martyrs, it also remembers the martyrs who stood fast in their faith unto death. If we become satisfied in our faith then we have not learned the lesson of Holy Scripture, that the "cloud of witnesses" include those who endured trials "of cruel mockings and scourgings," and those who were stoned, wandered in deserts and hid in caves. Wherefore, our faith is so tested as we look "unto Jesus the author and finisher of our faith." We are to seriously consider Christ who "endured such contradiction of sinners against himself, lest ye be wearied and faint in your minds." And

---

[1] Calvin, Institutes of the Christian Religion, F. L. Battles, Trans., Vol. 1, Book I, The Westminster Press, Philadelphia, 1973, page 224.

[2] Rev. Robert Simpson, Traditions of the Covenanters, ibid, page 215.

then this comment which should drive us to our knees and to His word: "Ye have not yet resisted unto blood, striving against sin."[1]

When the Beloved Apostle, John, saw the Lamb of God open the fifth seal, an altar was before him. Under this altar were "the souls of them that were slain for the Word of God, and for the testimony which they held." [Revelation 6:9].[2] Even today the saints of the Almighty King of kings are persecuted, jailed, and killed because of the Word of God. The question is asked from generation to generation, "How long, O Lord, holy and true, dost Thou not judge and avenge our blood on them that dwell on the earth?" [6:10]. The answer is given in the giving of white robes to each and every one of them, "that they should rest yet for a little season, until their fellow servants and also their brethren, who were to be killed as they were, should have fulfilled their course" [6:11].

John, on the Isle of Patmos, wrote that which the Spirit gave him, preparing the Lord's people for the sure coming promise recorded in Luke [21:20-22], "And when ye shall see Jerusalem compassed with armies, then know that the desolation thereof is nigh. Then let them which are in Judea flee to the mountains; and let them which are in the midst of it depart out; and let not them that are in the countries enter thereunto; for these be the days of vengeance, that all things which are written be fulfilled." David Chilton gave us these words to think about our need to be faithful and strong today, "That this blunt cry for vengeance strikes us as strange just shows how far our pietistic age has degenerated from the Biblical worldview. If our churches were more acquainted with the foundational hymnbook of the Church, the Psalms, instead of the sugary, syrupy, sweetness-and-light choruses that characterize modern evangelical hymnals, we would understand this much easier. But we have fallen under a pagan delusion that it is somehow "unchristian" to pray for God's wrath to be poured out upon the enemies and persecutors of the Church. Yet that is what we see God's people doing, with God's approval, in both Testaments of the Holy Scriptures. It is, in fact, a characteristic of the godly man that he despises the reprobate (Ps. 15:4). The spirit expressed in the imprecatory

---

[1] Hebrews 11:36-12:4.

[2] "Thus the breaking of the Fifth Seal reveals a scene from heaven, where the souls of those who had been slain are underneath, or around the base of, the altar. The image is taken from the Old Testament sacrifices, in which the blood of the slain victim would stream down the sides of the altar and form into a pool around its base ('the soul [Heb. *Nephesh*] of the flesh is in the *blood*,' Lev. 17:11)." The blood of the martyrs has been poured out (cf. 2 Tim. 4:6), and as it fills the trench below the altar it cries out from the ground with a loud voice, saying, How long, O Lord, holy and true, dost Thou not judge and avenge our blood upon those who dwell in the Land" –David Chilton, The Days of Vengeance, Dominion Press, Horn Lake, MS, pages 193-194.

prayers of Scripture is a necessary aspect of the Christian's attitude (cf. 2 Tim. 4:14). Much of the impotence of the churches today is directly attributable to the fact that they have become emasculated and effeminate. Such churches, unable even to confront evil—much less "overcome" it—will eventually be captured and dominated by their enemies."[1]

Hope in times of persecution rests in the Providence of God. Boettner quotes Calvin, "But God, who once commanded light to shine out of darkness, can marvelously bring, if He pleases, salvation out of hell itself, and thus turn darkness itself into light. But what worketh Satan? In a certain sense, the work of God! That is, God, by holding Satan fast bound in obedience to His Providence, turns him whithersoever He will, and thus applies the great enemy's devices and attempts to the accomplishment of His own eternal principles." Boettner continues, "Even the persecutions which are permitted to come upon the righteous are designed for good purposes. Paul declares that 'our light affliction, which is for a moment, worketh for us more and more exceedingly an eternal weight of glory,' II Cor. 4:17. To suffer with Christ is to be more closely united to Him, and great reward in heaven is promised to those who suffer in His behalf (Matt. 5:10-12)."[2]

When we look at history as the divine action of the Creator, we begin to understand the reality of prayer. Prayer is an action of the Almighty God in calling us to His throne of grace. John Calvin reminds us the Lord "opens to us the heavenly treasures that our whole faith may contemplate his beloved Son, our whole expectation depend on him, and our whole hope cleave to and rest in him;" that "just as faith is born from the gospel, so through it our hearts are trained to call upon God's name (Rom. 10:14-17)." Therefore, prayer was necessary in the lives of the Martyrs to obtain the promised strength of Christ in their faithful preaching of the Gospel. Calvin speaks to this, that "the Heavenly Father affirms that the only stronghold of safety is in calling upon his name (cf. Joel 2:32). By so doing we invoke the presence both of his providence, through which he watches over and guards our affairs, and of his power, through which he sustains us, weak as we are and well-nigh overcome, and of his goodness, through which he receives us, miserably burdened with sins, unto grace; and, in short, it is by prayer that we call him to reveal himself as wholly present to us."[3]

---

[1] David Chilton, ibid, pages 194-195.

[2] Ibid, pages 232-233.

[3] Calvin: Institutes of the Christian Religion, John T. McNeill, ed, in two volumes, The Westminster Press, Philadelphia, 1973, pages 850-851.

Worship the Lord

"How shall we describe his *revenues*—the honor, and glory, and worship, and respect, and esteem, and constant obedience, which he exacts as tribute from all the subjects of his dominion? 'He is the Lord, and worship thou him' (Ps. 45:11). 'Give unto the Lord the glory due his name: and bring an offering, and come into his courts. O worship the Lord in the beauty of holiness: fear before him all the earth' (Ps. 96:8-9). And all the royal *prerogatives* of apprehending and liberating, of condemning and acquitting, of life and death, of pardon and execution, belong to him without reserve: 'I kill and I make alive: I wound and I heal: neither is there any that can deliver out of my hand' (Deut. 32:39)."

Such, if we may so speak, are the *insignia* of the Mediator, insignia of transcendent value and matchless splendor. No titles like his titles; no throne of such peerless majesty; no crown of such overpowering radiance; no scepter of such resistless might; no laws so equitable or beneficent; no retinue so large or so illustrious; no ministers so dignified; no revenues so rich; no prerogatives so absolute, as his! 'Who in the heaven can be compared to the Lord? Who among the sons of the mighty can be likened unto him?'"

–William Symington, <u>Messiah the Prince</u>.[1]

---

[1] William Symington, <u>Messiah the Prince</u>, The Christian Statesman Press, Pittsburgh, Pa., 1999, page 18.

Robert Blair
He showed men the majesty of God

There was a London merchant who came to St. Andrews in Fife. By God's grace he heard three of Scotland's great preachers, Blair, Rutherford, and Dickson. He described the stature of Robert Blair, saying, "That man showed me the majesty of God." Of Samuel Rutherford he spoke, "that man showed me the loveliness of Christ." This merchant then heard the man with the long beard, David Dickson, responding, "That man showed me all my heart."

We would be blessed with ministers of the Word, who preach "the majesty of God, the loveliness of Christ, and the sins and sorrows of the human heart." For this was the central Biblical message that kept the church fed through both the peaceful and "Killing" times. These Covenanters were also the true patriots. They sought to honor God in both church and country. When King Charles took the road that belonged to King Jesus, they sought at any cost to vindicate the rights of the better Monarch. Along with their Puritan contemporaries in England, they wanted their congregations to understand the Word of God. They were true expositors of the Word, moving from chapter to chapter, verse by verse, preaching that which was more precious than gold and sweeter than honey.

Robert Blair was such a man, though he had to be tried in the fire of persecution before peers and king. Near the end of his life, his son David asked, ". . . now sir, God having given you time for after-thoughts on your way, we would hear what they are now?" He answered, "I have again and again thought upon my former ways, and communed with my heart; and as for my public actings and carriage, in reference to the Lord's work, if I were to begin again, I would just do as I have done." Robert loved to repeat Psalms 16 and 23, calling Psalm 71 his own. He died August 27, 1666.

Robert Blair was born at Irvine in 1593. His father, John Blair died when he was young, leaving his mother, Beatrix with six children. He was a good student, studying hard at the college of Glasgow (1608-). He testified that it pleased the Lord to visit him with fevers for a full four months, lest he should become puffed up with his proficiency. Robert finished his studies in Philosophy, revealing great skills in Humanity. He was encouraged to read the classical authors, beginning with Plautus. The Lord diverted him from this path as he read Augustine, finding in his Confession admonishment against the education of youth in heathen writings. He pursued in the reading of the Holy Scriptures and the ancient fathers of the faith.

In 1616 Mr. Blair entered on the trials for the ministry and was licensed to preach in the College Kirk. Some time after as regent in the College a loud cry sent him on a new search of Scriptures. The sound was, "The just shall live by faith!" He became acquainted with Mr. Culverwell's Treatise on Faith, which was of the same nature published by the Westminster Assembly.[1] He rejoiced in the truth of true faith which led him to appropriate the grace of God in Christ, to be guided more and more by the Holy Spirit, and in finding much comfort in his troubles. He witnesses: "About that time the Lord set me a work to stir up the students who were under my discipline earnestly to study piety, and to be diligent in secret seeking of the Lord; and my gracious Lord was pleased herein to bless my endeavors."

Robert Blair was ordained to the ministry in 1623. His first congregation was about 1200, in Bangor, Ireland. One of His struggles was over the expository preaching of the word of God or finding some interesting topic. He was led always to "go back unto that inexhaustible fountain of consolation." In the year 1646 the General Assembly at Edinburgh sent Robert Blair (then Moderator) along with Andrew Cant and Robert Douglas, to meet with Alexander Henderson who was laboring to convince King Charles I of the great bloodshed in the kingdoms. They tried to convince the King to be reconciled to the Presbyterian government and the Covenants. Though Mr. Blair was appointed as chaplain in Scotland and had a good standing with the King, the King would not subscribe to the Covenants and abolish Episcopacy in England. Mr. Blair responded, "Then you have not only defended it to the utmost of your power, but so long, and so far, that now you have no power." Sorrowfully he returned to St. Andrews.

Robert Blair was soon to be confined to his chamber in Edinburgh, rooted out by those who wanted a return to the Episcopacy and its related doctrines and leaders. He became sick and was allowed to retire to Inveresk about January of 1662. Robert endeared himself to the people

---

[1] "1. Those whom God effectually calleth, He also freely justifieth: not by infusing righteousness into them, but by pardoning their sins, and by accounting and accepting their persons as righteous, not for anything wrought in them, or done by them, but for Christ's sake alone; nor by imputing faith itself, the act of believing, or any other evangelical obedience to them, as their righteousness, but by imputing the obedience and satisfaction of Christ unto them, they receiving and resting on Him and His righteousness by faith; which faith they have not of themselves, it is a gift of God. 2. Faith, thus receiving and resting on Christ and His righteousness, is the alone instrument of justification; yet it is not alone in the person justified, but it is ever accompanied with all other saving graces, and is no dead faith, but worketh by love. 3. Christ, by His obedience and death, did fully discharge the debt of all those that are thus justified, and did make a proper, real, and full satisfaction to His Father's justice in their behalf. Yet, inasmuch as He was given by the Father for them; and His obedience and satisfaction accepted in their stead; and both freely, not for anything in them; their justification is only of free grace; that both the exact justice, and rich grace of God, might be glorified in the justification of sinners." –Westminster Confession of Faith (1647), chapter XI Of Justification.

of the church and of the country in which he lived, besides being a distinguished and appreciated part of the church court. He was a faithful minister of his Savior and King, Jesus, who with diligence and in his countenance, showed men the majesty of God.

His Glory Do Declare
PSALM 96[1]

O sing a new song to the Lord: sing all the earth to God.
To God sing, bless his name, shew still his saving health abroad.
Among the heathen nations his glory do declare;
And unto all the people shew his works that wondrous are.
For great's the Lord, and greatly to be magnify'd;
Yea, worthy to be fear'd is he above all gods beside.
For all the gods are idols dumb, which blinded nations fear;
But our God is the Lord, by whom the heav'ns created were.
Great honour is before his face, and majesty divine;
Strength is within his holy place, and there doth beauty shine.
Do ye ascribe unto the Lord, of people every tribe,
Glory do ye unto the Lord, and mighty pow'r ascribe.
Give ye glory to the Lord that to his name is due;
Come ye into his courts, and bring an offering with you.
In beauty of his holiness, O do the Lord adore;
Likewise let all the earth throughout tremble his face before.
Among the heathen say, God reigns; the world shall stedfastly
Be fix'd from moving; he shall judge the people righteously.
Let heav'ns be glad before the Lord, and let the earth rejoice;
Let seas, and all that is therein, cry out, and make a noise.
Let fields rejoice, and everything that springeth of the earth:
Then woods and ev'ry tree shall sing with gladness and with mirth
Before the Lord; because he comes, to judge the earth comes he:
He'll judge the world with righteousness, the people faithfully.

---

[1] Scottish Metrical Version; The Comprehensive Psalter, Blue Banner Books, Rowlett, Texas.

John Frith
Suffered Martyrdom with Great Courage

"The books that were written by this blessed martyr were many, and such sought after in the reign of King Edward the Sixth and Queen Elizabeth, for the instruction and comfort of the godly. He much helped Tindal in the translation of the New Testament. He suffered martyrdom, with great courage and a most forgiving spirit in 1531. – 'When he and another martyr were at the stake, doctor Cook, a priest in London, openly admonished the people, that they should in no wise pray for them–no more than they would do for a dog. At which words, Frith, smiling, desired the Lord to forgive them. These words did not a little move the people unto anger, and not without good cause. The wind made his death somewhat the longer, which bore away the flame from him unto his fellow that was burning with him; but he had established his mind with such patience, God giving him strength, that, even as though he had felt no pain in that long torment, he seemed rather to rejoice for his fellow, than to be careful for himself. This, truly, is the power and strength of Christ, striving and vanquishing in his saints; who sanctify us together with them, and direct us in all things to the glory of his most holy name. Amen.'"[1]

---

[1] <u>Accounts of Revival</u>, John Gillies, The Banner of Truth Trust, 1981, page 49.

James Mitchell
Jealous for the Lord God of hosts

James Mitchell was educated at the University of Edinburgh. Soon after the Restoration he received a license to preach the Gospel. He joined with the faithful few in 1666 against the tyranny of Charles II and Prelacy.

The archenemy of the Presbyterians and Covenanters was Archbishop Sharp. He was seen as a traitor and apostate who would do anything to rid Scotland of the Presbyterians. James Mitchell saw Sharp as the main instigator of oppression and persecution. He took his zeal to the very coach of the Archbishop. On July 11, 1668, he waited for Sharp to come down to his coach. On this day Sharp was accompanied by Honeyman, Bishop of Orkney. As the Archbishop took his seat in the coach, Mitchell stepped out of hiding and discharged his pistol, loaded with three balls. Honeyman, who was setting his foot in the boot of the coach, reached his hand up and was shot in the wrist. The Primate escaped the shots.

Mitchell escaped to a house and changed his clothes. On Monday the thirteenth the Council issued a proclamation, offering a reward of 5,000 merks to anyone, who would discover the person who shot the Bishop. The Council used this occasion to publish a scurrilous pamphlet against the Presbyterian Church of Scotland. Lies abounded against Alexander Henderson, David Dickson, and James Mitchell.

In 1674 Mitchell was discovered by Sir William Sharp, the Archbishop's brother. On the tenth of February James was examined by the Lord Chancellor. He confessed to the shooting on the promise that his life would be spared. But this was not to be. He would be examined by torture concerning the rebellion of 1666. He spent two years at the tollbooth (prison). In 1676 he was again brought before the Council to be examined for his part in the insurrection. At one meeting the "boots" were placed before Mitchell and the President of the Council said, "You see what is on the table; I will see if that will make you do it."

Part of Mitchell's testimony before the Council, reads, "I confess that by torture you may cause me to blaspheme God, . . . I here protest before God and your lordships, that nothing thus extorted from me shall be made use of against me in judgment . . . I am so much a Christian, that whatever your lordships shall legally prove against me, if it be a truth I shall not deny it; but, on the other hand, I am so much a Scotsman, that I can never hold myself obliged by the law of God, nature, or the nation, to become my own accuser."

While Mitchell was in prison he gave this cause for his suffering, "I have been very jealous for the Lord God of hosts" (referring to 1 Kings 19:4). He adhered to the covenanted work of Reformation and the Covenants, and approved of such works as Lex Rex by Rutherford. On January 18, 1678, he was brought to the Grassmarket of Edinburgh and executed. With the exception of that one act that cannot ·be fully condoned, James Mitchell was a man who was known for his zeal for the faith, and for his Christian piety.

Bishop Sharp was undoubtedly one of the chief instigators of tyranny and bloodshed during these killing times in Scotland. Mitchell thought he had every right to get rid of this enemy of Christ. He said this of Sharp: "For I, by his instigation, being excluded from all grace and favor, thought it my duty to pursue him on all occasion."

There is singular consolation, moreover, when we are persecuted for righteousness' sake. For our thought should then be, How high the honor which God bestows upon us in distinguishing us by the special badge of his soldiers. By suffering persecution for righteousness' sake, I mean not only striving for the defense of the Gospel, but for the defense of righteousness in any way. Whether, therefore, in maintaining the truth of God against the lies of Satan, or defending the good and innocent against the injuries of the bad, we are obliged to incur the offense and hatred of the world, so as to endanger life, fortune, or honor, let us not grieve or decline so far to spend ourselves for God; let us not think ourselves wretched in those things in which he with his own lips has pronounced us blessed (Matthew 5:10.)   -John Calvin, Institutes

"My grace is sufficient for thee; for my strength is made perfect in weakness."
Christ our Lord and Savior

Robert Boyd
He bears the cross with joy

Robert Boyd of Trochrig was born at Glasgow in the year 1578. This was the time of James VI. It was during his reign that, in 1618, the Five Articles of Perth was adopted by the General Assembly. King James called the Assembly together on August 25. The Prelates were in full control, along with the nobility and gentry. The ministers of Scotland had to stand in the rear. Spottiswoode claimed the right to preside as moderator as it was held in his diocese. When it came time to vote on the Articles, Spottiswoode announced that the vote would be taken down along with all the names of those voting against the Articles. These names would be sent to the King.

The Five Articles of Perth was ratified by the Parliament in 1621. They were to be enforced by the Court of High Commission, and those who refused to carry out its provision would face civil penalties. King James wrote to the Prelates that the sword was now in their hands, and they should not let it rust. The articles contained, in part, Communion to be received in a kneeling posture, private communion in case of sickness, private baptism in cases of necessity, catechizing young people and their being blessed by Bishops. Holy days were affirmed to be for the "whole Kirk of the World." Throughout Scotland theirs was a cry of indignation, for these Articles were made not only the law of the Church but the law of the land.

Robert Boyd traveled to France at an early age, becoming the professor of divinity of Saumur. Invited by King James VI to return to Scotland, he became principal of the College at Glasgow and minister of Govan. Boyd's sermons were written out in full. However, his pulpit preaching was full of life and power. As the Church of Scotland took a lot of his time, he became a zealous friend and supporter of the faithful ministers of the Word.

The prelatists respected Robert Boyd and the other ministers for their piety, learning, and place of influence. The bishops labored diligently to get Boyd to come to their side. He gave-in to the extent that he gave a paper to Archbishop Law of Glasgow, in which he seemed to acknowledge the preeminence of bishops. Finding no rest for his soul on that evening, Robert Boyd sought to have his paper returned. The Archbishop pretended that the paper was already on its way to the King.

Finding no peace in Glasgow Boyd demitted both his charges,

becoming principal of the college of Edinburgh in October of 1622. Among the ministers of that city who envied Robert Boyd as a preacher and teacher was a man by the name of Andrew Ramsay. Ramsay sent the King a letter informing him that Boyd was a nonconformist. The King issued a command to the magistrates that Boyd be removed from his positions. The magistrates requested that the King reconsider and allow Boyd to remain in Edinburgh. The King, on the last day of January 1623, renewed his order to have him removed.

Later, Archbishop Law was prevailed on to admit Mr. Boyd to be a minister of Paisley. This was done, even though Boyd was opposed to the Perth Articles, having refused conformity to them both at Glasgow and Edinburgh. It was his learning and prudence that recommended him to the Archbishop.

At Paisley Robert Boyd remained at peace until the brother of the Earl of Abercorn, a zealous Papist, went to the church to dispossess him. On a Sabbath afternoon, while Boyd was preaching, the Earl threw all of his books out of his house of residence. Boyd complained to the Privy Council and the offender was imprisoned. The man professed his sorrow for what he had done, and Robert Boyd interceded for him. However, when Mr. Boyd went back to the church he found the doors secured. A mob pressed so hard on Robert Boyd, with contemptuous speeches and by the throwing of stones, he was soon forced to flee to Glasgow.

Robert Boyd returned to his own house at Trochrig in Carrick. He died on January 5, 1627. His life was tempered to the cross of His Savior. It was said that he bore the cross with much joy. His commentary on Ephesians testifies to his learning. He would sometimes say that if he had his choice of languages, in which he would deliver his messages, it would be Greek. He looked for the grace of God in others, esteeming them higher than himself. He gave many thanks for the work of the grace of Christ in others.

"Most gladly therefore will I rather glory in my infirmities, that the power of Christ may rest upon me. Therefore I take pleasure in infirmities, in reproaches, in necessities in persecutions, in distresses for Christ's sake; for when I am weak, then I am strong."
–Paul; 2 Cor. 12:9-10

Donald Cargill
From the scaffold, this 'Scots Worthy' sang from Psalm 118,
"The Lord is my strength and song, and is become my salvation."

Donald Cargill was born about the year 1619, the eldest son of a respected family in the parish of Rattray of Perthshire. His father urged him to study for the ministry. He felt that the burden of the ministry was too much for him to bear until, after much prayer, these words of Ezekiel were etched on his heart, "Son of man, eat this roll, and go speak unto the house of Israel." Donald Cargill then dedicated his life wholly to the ministry of the Word. It was said of Cargill that though he was timid and disposed to self-depreciation, "nevertheless he kept the flag flying when others were too panic-stricken to unfurl its folds."

He was licensed by the Presbytery, and asked to preach on Ezekiel 3:1. Doing so, his call was further affirmed by God in his heart. He received a call to the Barony Church at Glasgow. However, he felt that the people were too rebellious of heart and unconcerned toward the Word. In vain his fellow ministers urged him to stay. As he was getting his horse ready for travel, a godly woman pleaded with him, "Sir, you have promised to preach on Thursday; have you appointed a meal for starving people, and will you go away and not give it? If you do, the curse of God will go with you." His heart pierced, he continued to preach and exercise his ministry to both his parish and beyond.

The ministry of the Word soon would be challenged by the restoration of Charles II, Prelacy being restored again. May 29, 1660 was set apart to celebrate the return of Charles II to the throne. Cargill preached to a large crowed at the Barony Kirk. Faithfully he preached the Word of God. Speaking of the king, he said, with tears in his eyes, "We thought once to have blessed the day wherein the king came home again; but now we think we should have reason to curse it." He spoke of the king as "wofullest sight that ever the poor Church of Scotland saw."

This enraged the enemy. Hotly pursued, Cargill hid in private homes and in the brush of the country. He continued his ministry with the preaching of the word, catechizing the children, and visiting the families. The darkness continued to spread with the act of council, 1662, whereby Presbyterians were to be removed from the churches. Soldiers were sent to imprison Cargill, but they could not find him.

Preaching in the fields of Scotland caused his voice to become weak. One day a Mr. Blackader was invited to preach and Cargill desired to preach with him. Cargill chose his text, Isaiah 44:3, "I will pour water on him that is thirsty." The heart of the people went with him, knowing the soreness of his voice. However, the Lord was pleased to clear his voice and enlarge his spirit. Succeeding him, Blackader said, "Ye, that have such preaching, have no need to invite strangers to preach to you; make good use of your mercy." Cargill narrowly escaped the armies of the king. Once, while riding by a band of Musketeers, he was asked the time. Answering, his voice was recognized, but his horse carried him to safety. Another remarkable escape came in a house in the city. The army searched the house from top to bottom. So thorough was their search that as they looked through the loft they fell through the ceiling. However, if they had looked behind the books which covered a window, they would have discovered Cargill and a friend.

Cargill spoke of himself, when near death, saying, "I have followed holiness; I have taught truth." His sermons being shorter, as well as his prayers in worship, than most of the brothers in the Word, he was once asked, "O, sir, 'tis long betwixt meals, and we are in a starving condition. All is good, sweet, and wholesome, which ye deliver; but why do you straiten us so much with shortness?" To which he answered, "Ever since I bowed a knee in good earnest to pray, I never durst pray and preach with my gifts; and where my heart is not affected, and comes not up with my mouth, I always thought it time for me to quit it. What comes not from my heart, I have little hope that it will go to the heart of others." Though Donald Cargill did not weary his listeners with long prayers, he did not weary in his private devotions. It is said that in both families and in secret, Cargill "sat straight upon his knees, without resting upon anything, with his hands lifted up; and some took notice he died the same way, with the bloody rope about his neck." Alexander Smellie wrote of Cargill, "Happy man, to live and to die in perfect familiarity of trust with his King and Friend."

Cargill continued to faithfully minister the Word until he was taken a prisoner on the night of July 10, 1681. On July 15 he stood before Chancellor Rothes who ranted and raved against him. Cargill replied, "My Lord Rothes, forbear to threaten me, for die what death I will, your eyes shall not see it." It came to pass that Rothes died on the morning of the day Cargill was to be hung.

This was a year after Donald Cargill preached the funeral sermon of Richard Cameron, having chosen the text, "Know ye not that there is a prince and a great man fallen this day in Israel?" Cameron, called the "Lion of the Covenant," died at the age of thirty-two, with a fight with Strachan's dragoons. Cameron looked to this battle with these words, "For this is the day that I have longed for, to die fighting against our Lord's enemies; and this is the day that we will get the crown."

On the scaffold Cargill answered his indictment by pointing to the Advocate Sir George M'Kenzie as the man "who took the Holy Bible in his hand, and said, it would never be well with the land, until the book was destroyed." This is in contrast to Cargill's hope in Christ as the one who would redeem Scotland. Among his words to the people from the scaffold were these: "Now, I am as sure of my interest in Christ and peace with God, as all within this Bible and the Spirit of God can make me; and I am fully persuaded this is the very way for which I suffer, and that He will return gloriously to Scotland."

On the 26th of July Cargill was condemned, and he was executed on the 27th of July, 1681. From the scaffold he sang from Psalm 118,

The right hand of the mighty Lord
Exalted on high;
The right hand of the mighty Lord
Doth ever valiantly.
Thou art my God, I'll Thee exalt,
My God I will Thee praise;
Give thanks to God for He is good,
His mercy lasts always.

Rev. Carslaw sums up the life of Donald Cargill with these words, "Cargill was a man of his own time, as we all are, circumscribed in thought and action by the ideas and spirit of his age, and therefore liable in some respects to be misjudged by us, and to be unjustly condemned for unreasonable obstinacy and intolerance. But in spite of much imperfection, which no one would have been more ready to acknowledge than himself, we hear in his earnest contendings, even unto death, the eternal voice of humanity every struggling against tyranny, which is of the devil, and for liberty, which is of God. And we are not worthy of the noble heritage, which he and others by their faithfulness have secured and handed down to us, unless, when the occasion calls for it, we too are willing to suffer the loss of all things for the excellency of the knowledge of Christ Jesus our Lord!"[1]

---

[1] W. H. Carslaw, <u>Life and Times of Donald Cargill</u>, Paisley Alexander Gardner, Publisher by Appointment to the late Queen Victoria, page 131.

An Acrostic on the name of Donald Cargill[1]

Most sweet and savoury is thy fame,
And more renowned is thy name,
Surely, than any can record,
Thou highly favoured of the Lord!
Exalted thou on earth didst live;
Rich grace to thee the Lord did give.

During the time thou dwelt'st below,
On in a course to heaven didst go.
Not casten down with doubts and fears,
Assured of heaven near thirty years,
Labour thou didst in Christ's vineyard;
Diligent wast, not time thou spar'd.

Christ's standard thou didst bear alone,
After others from it were gone,
Right zeal for truth was found in thee,
Great sinners censur'd'st faithfully.
In holding truth didst constant prove,
Laidst down thy life out of true love.

Be Strong in the Lord and in the Authority of His Might!

"Put on the whole armor of God, that ye may be able to stand against the wiles of the devil. For we wrestle not against flesh and blood, but against principalities, against powers, against the rulers of darkness of this world, against spiritual wickedness in high places. Therefore, take unto the whole armor of God, that ye may be able to withstand in the evil day, and having done all to stand."

–Ephesians 6:11-13

---

[1] John Howie, <u>The Scots Worthies</u>, Oliphant, Anderson & Ferrier, London, page 453.

Grisell Hume
Lady Baille of Jerviswood
"Her hospitality never wavered."

Grisell Hume was born at Redbraes Castle in Berwickshire, December 25, 1665. Her father was Sir Patrick Hume, and her mother, Grisell Kerr of Sr. Thomas Kerr of Cavers. Grisell was the eldest child of eighteen children. Her father distinguished himself as a patriot and a statesman. Sir Patrick suffered for his faith. In 1674 he went to London with the Duke of Hamilton and others to lay before the council the sufferings of the nation under the Administration of the Duke of Lauderdale.

In 1675 the Privy Council appointed garrisons to be placed in certain homes of noblemen and gentlemen for the purpose of suppressing conventicles. Several shires refused to contribute to the food and housing of the garrisons, sending Sir Patrick Hume with a complaint to the council. Hume was imprisoned in September of 1675. A letter dated October fifth from his majesty approved his imprisonment and commanded the council to declare Hume as incapable of public trust. Sir Patrick was in prison until the King gave orders for his release in a letter dated February 24, 1676. Lady Grisell thus began her life during the troubles of persecution. She was ten years of age when her father was released from prison. She had tenacity beyond her years which helped her accomplish many confidential missions given to her by her parents.

When Robert Baille of Jerviswood, an early friend of her father's, was imprisoned for rescuing his brother-in-law, James Kirkten, from a wicked persecutor, Lady Grisell was sent by her father to Edinburgh. There, because of her age, she managed to get admitted to the prison, unsuspected, to slip a letter of information and advice to Robert Baille. She was able to return to her parents with intelligence information.

It was at this prison that Grisell first set eyes on Mr. Baille's son, George. The romance began which afterwards would result in marriage. Many more adventures were Lady Grisell's

as her parents continued to employ her as a secret messenger. In July of 1678 her father was again made a prisoner in the tollbooth of Edinburgh. He was later sent to Dumbarton Castle. Grisell made repeated visits to her father, comforting him and giving to him intelligence reports.

In October of 1682 Robert Baille was caught in London and sent to Scotland for imprisonment. He was much comforted by the Word of God. The Psalms of David was a rich treasure to him as to the heavenly instruction and comfort. He had memorized the Psalms in Latin. He was blessed as he joyfully repeated the Psalms in the dark and weary hours of his confinement.

Sir Patrick's estate was forfeited to the crown. Grisell went with her mother to London hoping to obtain an allowance out of her husband's estate, for herself and her 10 children. She was able to get $150 pounds per year. They went to Holland to be with their father and husband. Grisell returned to Scotland to be with her sister, Julian, in her sickness. When she was well enough, they traveled to Holland, where they spent more than three years.

George Baille was also a refugee in Holland at the time that Sir Patrick and his family were there. The love between George and Grisell was growing, though their finances held them back from any commitment. Grisell had offers from others of means, but refused them all. The family returned to Scotland and soon found favor from King William. The estates were returned to the families. Robert and Grisell were married on September 17, 1692. Lady Baille kept her buoyant spirit and humor, which is said to be part of the Presbyterian and Covenanter spirit. Her hospitality never wavered for all who were in need, rich or poor.

Lady Baille lost her mother in 1703. She also cared for and comforted her father throughout his life. Her husband, George Baille, died on August 6, 1738. She spoke of him as "the best of husbands, and delight of my life for forty-eight years." Lady Baille died on December 6, 1746. It was written of Lady Baille that she "would have made a most able and magnanimous queen." The following inscription in marble, which is set above her monument, speaks of her gracious character charting the most singular events of her life:

"HERE LIETH[1] **The Right Honourable Lady Grisell Baillie,** wife of George Baillie of Jerviswood, Esq., eldest daughter of the Right Honourable Patrick, Earl of Marchmont; a pattern to her sex, and an honour to her country. She excelled in the character of a daughter, a wife, a mother. While an infant, at the hazard of her own, she preserved her father's life; who under the rigorous persecution of arbitrary power, sought refuge in the close

---

[1] James Anderson, <u>Ladies of the Covenant</u>, Blackie & Son, Edinburgh, pages 586-587.

confinement of a tomb, where he was nightly supplied with necessities, conveyed by her with a caution far above her years, a courage almost above her sex; a real instance of the so much celebrated Roman charity. She was a shining example of conjugal affection, that knew no dissension, felt no decline, during almost a fifty years union; the dissolution of which she survived from duty, not choice. Her conduct as a parent was amiable, exemplary, and successful, to a degree not well to be expressed, without mixing the praises of the dead with those of the living; who desire that all praise, but of her, should be silent. At different times she managed the affairs of her father, her husband, her family, her relations, with unwearied application, with happy economy, as distant from avarice as from prodigality. Christian piety, love of her country, zeal for her friends, compassion for her enemies, cheerfulness of spirit, pleasantness of conversation, dignity of mind, good breeding, good humour, good sense, wee the daily ornaments of an useful life, protracted by Providence to an uncommon length, for the benefit of all who fell within the sphere of her benevolence. Full of years, and of good works, she died on the 6th day of December 1746, near the end of her 81st year, and was buried on her birth day, the 25th of that month."

Given to Hospitality

"Let love be without dissimulation. Abhor that which is evil; cleave to that which is good. Be kindly affectioned one to another with brotherly love; in honor preferring one another; not slothful in business; fervent in spirit; serving the Lord; rejoicing in hope; patient in tribulation; continuing instant in prayer. Bless them which persecute you; bless, and curse not. Rejoice with them that do rejoice, and weep with them that weep. Be of the same mind one toward another. Mind not high things, but condescend to men of low estate. Be not wise in your own conceits. Recompense to no man evil for evil. Provide things honest in the sight of all men."

--Romans 12:9-17

Of Good Works[1]

These good works, done in obedience to God's commandments, are the fruits and evidences of a true and lively faith: and by them believers manifest their thankfulness, strengthen their assurance, edify their brethren, adorn the profession of the gospel, stop the mouths of the adversaries, and glorify God, whose workmanship they are, created in Christ Jesus thereunto; that, having their fruit unto holiness, they may have the end, eternal life.

Man's Sanctification and Good Works[2]

Therefore it is impossible that this holy faith can be unfruitful in man; for we do not speak of a vain faith as is called in Scripture *a faith that worketh by love*, which excites man to the practice of those works which God has commanded in His Word. Which works, as they proceed from the good root of faith, are good and acceptable in the sight of God, forasmuch as they are all sanctified by His grace; howbeit they are of no account towards our justification. For it is by faith in Christ we are justified, even before we do good works, any more than the fruit of a tree can be good before the tree itself is good.

---

[1] Westminster Confession of Faith, ibid, Of Good Works, pages 68-69. "Herein is my Father glorified, that ye bear much fruit; so shall ye be my disciples" [Christ, John 15:8]. "For we are his workmanship, created in Christ Jesus unto good works, which God hath before ordained that we should walk in them" [Eph. 2:10]. "But now being made free from sin, and become servants to God, ye have our fruit unto holiness, and the end everlasting life" [Rom. 6:22].

[2] Reformed Confessions Harmonized, Baker Books, Michigan, 1999, Belgic Confession, Article 24, page 114. "That being justified by his grace, we should be made heirs according to the hope of eternal life. This is a faithful saying, and these things I will that thou affirm constantly, that they which have believed in God might be careful to maintain good works. These things are good and profitable unto men" [Titus 3:7-8].

Lady Graden
A comforter worthy of praise

Helen Johnston was the daughter of Lord Warrington, who fell as a martyr to the cause of civil and religious freedom. He was once "trusted with the whole government of Scotland," however, he left but a small provision for his family and thirteen children. Lord Warrington was a man of God whose prayers were so intense and concentrated upon his heavenly Father that on one occasion his wife, having fainted, was carried from the room by her servants, without his knowing it.

Helen Johnston, however, enjoyed an inestimable blessing of a sound Christian education along with holy examples in the household. From the cradle she was surrounded with piety and a love for liberty. Helen witnessed the overthrow of the Presbyterian Church by the government of Charles II. This oppression sought to force the conscience of men and women to conform their religious beliefs to those of the monarch. This cruelty led to her witness of her father as he was led to the scaffold.

Helen was married in the summer of 1659 to Mr. George Hume, proprietor of Graden Estate in the south of Scotland. According to the courtesy of the times he was called Graden and his wife, Helen, Lady Graden. Mr. Hume was a warm supporter of the Covenanters, and came to suffer in their defense. In 1678 Graden was made a prisoner in Crockome, a village on the English border. It is not known how long he was kept a prisoner. However, his name was later found among those listed as rebels and traitors. He died in the year 1679.

Lady Graden rises in the history of the Covenanters in the year 1684 as a sufferer in the cause of Presbytery. She was tormented many times for her faith in Christ. Her primary enemy was Henry Ker of Graden, who, in 1684, held the office of Sheriff. He recklessly imposed exorbitant fines on the gentlemen and ladies who embraced the cause of nonconformity. Lady Graden revealed her Christian character of love and heroism that was observant in the ladies of the Covenant during these times of affliction. Her actions revealed sympathy, compassion, and a self-sacrificing spirit. This Christ-like spirit is shown in her relationship with her sister and brother-in-law, Robert Baillie of Jerviswood.

Robert Baillie, also her cousin, fell sickly while in prison for his faith. The grace of Lady Graden was shown as she ministered to his needs during this trying time. It is recorded that in the giving of comfort and grace she was worthy of all praise. Baillie, who experienced the work of the Holy Spirit from age ten, was a descendant of John Knox. His daily study and constant delight was Christ crucified. Around 1684 Baillie's illness took a turn for the worse. His wife and friends became troubled and anxious. His wife appealed to the council to let him out of prison that she could care for him at her quarters. But they were determined to keep him, with a covetous eye on his prize estates. Thus, she was refused. She wished to care for him at prison, but she herself became sick.

Lady Baillie of Jerviswood's sister, Lady Graden, sought to comfort her sister and cousin, seeking permission to attend the sick Robert Baillie. The council, finding Baillie dangerously ill, allowed her to attend him on certain conditions. These were: she had to remain a prisoner with him, she was to be searched for letters before entering his cell, and she could not leave without permission of the council. Later, Lady Jerviswood was allowed to visit her husband if she would come with the physician. She was only allowed to talk to her husband when the Physician was present.

She was later allowed to stay with Robert under the same rules as her sister. His cup of affliction was sweetened with the love and compassion of these two ladies. They comforted him with thoughts of Christ and faith. The three of them found

Lady Graden reading to Robert Baillie in Prison.

much enjoyment in this. A few weeks later the ladies were removed from prison, and for two months Robert was alone. Lady Graden returned after this period and remained with her cousin until his death. She continued to remind him of the promises and hope of the gospel, reading from the Book of God the lessons of comfort and teachings. Robert listened intently to every word of eternal glories.

Lady Graden took her place next to Robert Baillie when he was brought to trial on December 23. The jury was to bring in a verdict by nine the next morning. At ten o'clock he was sentenced to death at the market cross of Edinburgh, his head was to be cut off and displayed. Lady Graden's ability to comfort in time of greatest affliction came from the God of all comfort. She witnessed in her cousin an infirm body but not an infirm soul. She listened carefully to his last prayers full of salvation and triumphant faith. A shining majesty could be seen in his face as one in heaven, of the joy of meeting the saints with the Lord.

Robert Baillie was carried to the scaffold in a chair. Lady Graden walked alongside. As they passed by her father's house, they were reminded of his faith and sacrifice. She said to Baillie, "the same grace which supported him is able to support you." Lady Graden lived to see the Stuarts expelled from the British throne, and to rejoice in the deliverance affected by the Prince of Orange. She saw the descendants of Baillie raised to high honor and trust in the new government. The family continued to adorn their high stations with Christian virtues which distinguished their martyred father, which proved a blessing to their country in their day and generation. Lady Graden joined the saints in heaven on September 11, 1707.

Comfort in Tribulation

"Blessed be God, even the Father of our Lord Jesus Christ, the Father of mercies, and the God of all comfort; who comforteth us in all our tribulation, that we may be able to comfort them which are in any trouble, by the comfort wherewith we ourselves are comforted of God. For as the sufferings of Christ abound in us, so our consolation also aboundeth by Christ. And whether we be afflicted, it is for your consolation and salvation, which is effectual in the enduring of the same sufferings which we also suffer; or whether we be comforted, it is for your consolation and salvation. And our hope of you is steadfast, knowing, that as ye are partakers of the sufferings, so shall ye be also of the consolation. For we would not, brethren, have you ignorant of our trouble which came to us in Asia, that we were pressed out of measure, above strength, insomuch that we despaired even of life; but we had the sentence of death in ourselves, that we should not trust in ourselves, but in God which raiseth the dead; who delivered us from so great a death, and doth deliver; in whom we trust that he will yet deliver us."

–Paul, 2 Corinthians 1:3-10

The Noble Christian

A heart in heaven is *the highest excellence of Christian Temper.* As there is a common excellence, by which Christians differ from the world, so there is this peculiar dignity of spirit, by which the more excellent differ from the rest. As the noblest of creatures, so the noblest of Christians, are they whose faces are set most direct for heaven. Such a heavenly saint, who hath been wrapped up to God in his contemplations, and is newly come down from the views of Christ, what discoveries will he make of those superior regions! how high and sacred is his discourse! enough to convince an understanding hearer, that he hath seen the Lord, and that no man could speak such words, except he had been with God. This, is the noble Christian. The most famous mountains and trees are those that reach nearest to heaven; and he is the choicest Christian, whose heart is most frequently and most delightfully there. If a man have lived near the king, or hath seen the sultan of Persia, or the great Turk, he will be thought a step higher than his neighbors. What, then, shall we judge of him that daily travels as far as heaven, and there hath seen the King of kings, hath frequent admittance into the divine presence, and feasteth his soul upon the tree of life? For my part, I value this man before the noblest, the richest, the most learned, in the world.

–Richard Baxter[1]

---

[1] The Saints' everlasting rest, Richard Baxter, The National Foundation for Christian Education, Marshallton, Delaware, page 201.

James Renwick
Carried the Banner faithfully

It was written of James Renwick that he displayed the "banner of the Gospel faithfully in the dark cold stormy nights as well as in the day time, breaking the Bread of Life to his hearers."

Renwick, covenanter and Scots Worthy minister of the Word, carried his banner high so that both friend and foe could clearly see its glory. He preached, taught, wrote, and fought the battle for Christ in Scotland. He was the faithful under-shepherd of the sheep of the Good Shepherd, feeding them the Word of truth. His enemies referred to him as Field-preacher, Rebel, and Vagrant.

Renwick was born February 15, 1662 in the parish of Glencairn. His father, Andrew, was a weaver by trade. His mother, Elizabeth, after having several children who died, prayed for a child from the Lord, that a son would come, not only to be an heir of glory, but to live to serve the Lord. When James was born, she dedicated him to the Lord. James was inclined to pray at the early age of two, learning to read the Bible when six years old.

James Renwick was assaulted by the world's atheism and the unfaithfulness of the church's ministers. However, the Lord would not have His servant ignorant of His work on earth. James' faith was confirmed by faithful ministers such as Donald Cargill, minister and martyr of the Word. James saw in him the grace of God, and witnessed the steadfastness of true faith as he watched his execution on July 27, 1681. Renwick became more and more determined to witness for the cause of Christ, for which many suffered. His instruction came from the Word of God, as a strong hand which reached into his heart, a love which comforted his soul, so that the temptations, persecutions, ravings, and tribulations he faced, could not shake his faith nor bring doubt about his Lord, till the day of his death.

James was ordained in Holland, subscribing to the Confession and Catechism of the Church of Scotland. He would not subscribe to the corrupted catechisms which prevailed at that time. It was said of that solemn occasion that Renwick's face seemed to shine, being so filled with the Spirit of God. He began his work of ministry in Scotland in September of 1683, boldly taking up the standard of Christ the King.

As with other faithful ministers he had to bear the false witnesses as well as the armies of the king. The more he preached in the fields, the hotter the persecution followed him. Proclaimed a traitor and rebel, Renwick was motivated to proclaim the gospel with greater zeal. The more rigorously he was opposed, the more his followers increased. He warned vigorously against the proclamations of toleration, urging minister and people to stand firm in the true faith. From that time on he was truly a hunted man. Within a few months at least fifteen searches were made for him. One hundred-pound sterling was offered, dead or alive.

Our Lord chose February 17, 1688 as the day He would receive James Renwick into paradise. As his mother and young sisters visited him in the jail, he prayed with a hope only a child of God can have, "O! How can I contain this, to be within two hours of the crown of glory?" He looked forward to seeing his Lord.

To the very end his tormenters tried to dissuade him from his chosen course, to deny his Lord. James Renwick would hold his King's banner high until the Lord Himself would pass it onto another. His witness from the scaffold was both an appeal to the church and to the nation. We should so preach the gospel today, giving thanks for those who have gone on before, to glory of our King and His banner. Among other things, James said, "I am with a little to appear before Him who is King of kings, and Lord of lords, who shall pour shame, contempt and confusion upon all the kings of the earth who have not ruled for Him."

The Covenanters' Scaffold Song

> Sing with me, sing with me!
> Blessed spirits, sing with me;
> To the Lamb our song shall be
> Through a glad eternity,
> Farewell, earthly morn and even,
> Sun and moon and stars of heaven.
> Heavenly portals open before me;
> Welcome, Christ, in all Thy glory!
> Sing with me, sing with me, sing with me.
> Blessed spirits, sing with me.
> Ames Hogg

John Brown
A clear shining light

There was more than one John Brown whose "body lies amouldering in his grave while his soul goes marching on." Among the Covenanting Martyrs, John Brown of Priesthill was a faithful servant of Christ, who early felt the hatred of the enemies of His Lord. He came from the Shire of Ayr, a close friend of Alexander Peden and Richard Cameron. Peden, who was called "Prophet of the Covenant," spoke of Brown as "a clear shining light, the greatest Christian I ever conversed with."

 Alexander Peden married John Brown to Isabel Weir in the year 1682. To John Brown, Peden was a "taste of the world to come." After the simple ceremony Peden said to Isabel, "You have a good man; but you will not enjoy him long. Prize his company, and keep linen by you to be his winding sheet; for you will need it when you are not looking for it, and it will be a bloody one." John and Isabel would know but three years of blessing together. Their home was one of grace and love. John was a poor man as far as earthly goods were concerned. He never owned more than one cow and twenty sheep.

He had a desire for the ministry, but he had to give this up because of an impediment in his speech. However, he became a special blessing to the youth of the area. The young people came from miles around to John Brown's Bible school. John had his own rustic school of Theology. Some of the boys became martyrs at the hands of the king's army, for John taught the youth to resist evil and sin, even to the drawing of blood.

In the summer John would hold his Bible studies in the sheepfold. In the winter they gathered around the fire in the kitchen. It is said that John Brown was one of the first founders of Bible classes and Sunday schools. The heart of the Covenanters was directed to the lost souls of Scotland. They were hunted as wild animals as they faithfully preached and taught Christ.

The spirit of their mission is seen in these words, a part of their rules for Society Meetings: "As it is the undoubted duty of all to pray for the coming of Christ's kingdom, so all that love our Lord Jesus Christ in sincerity, and know what it is to bow a knee in good earnest, will long and pray for the out-making of the Gospel promises to His Church in the latter days, that King Christ would go out upon the white horse of the Gospel, conquering and to conquer, and make a conquest of the travail of His soul, that it may be sounded that the kingdoms of the world are become His, and His Name called upon from the rising of the sun to its going down."

There is no cottage to mark the spot where John and Isabel lived, where the family rose early each morning for worship. About five miles from the town of Moirkirk you will see a monument to John Brown.

In April of 1685 the hawks were looking for Alexander Peden and the boy Renwick. This honored friend, Peden, stayed with the Browns for an evening. One morning in May, after family worship, John Brown and his nephew went out to cut some peats. Claverhouse and his troops surrounded them, asking why prominent Covenanters visited them. Brown was asked to swear an oath of allegiance to the king. Brown refused to do so and the soldiers took them back to the house. At the door to his house Brown was questioned. John's stammering disappeared as he witnessed to his King and Savior. Claverhouse wanted nothing of this and made John go to his knees, allowing him to pray. Claverhouse told John, "Go to your prayers for you shall surely die." However, his prayers were of such a nature that John was interrupted several times. John was accused of preaching instead of praying. John continued his conversation with his Lord, asking for that precious remnant to be saved.

Claverhouse angrily commanded his troops to shoot John Brown on the spot. Some have written that the dragoons shot John Brown. Another account says that they refused to shoot and Claverhouse took his pistol and placed it to the head of John Brown, and shot him. This murder was witnessed by his wife. Isabel. Putting her child on the ground, she wrapped the head of her husband, sat by him and wept. Jean Brown, whose husband and two sons were shot because of their faith, came to Isabel and comforted her.

The Death of John Brown

> The child on the moss she laid
> And she stretched the cold limbs of the dead,
> And drew the eyelid's shade,
> And bound the corpses shattered head,
> And shrouded the martyr in his plaid;
> And where the dead and living slept,
> Sat in the wilderness and wept.
>
>   –Henry Inglis

John Brown was the priceless jewel of Isabel's life. She willingly gave him up to the company of witnesses with whom he would feel much at home. She faithfully brought up her children in the way of the Lord. She continued the witness of her husband as she encouraged the godly and comforted the mourner with the comfort wherewith she had been comforted by her Lord.

    About a mile from the farm of Priesthill is the grave of John Brown. Its grave slab reads:

> In death's cold bed the dusty part here lies
> Of one who did the earth as dust despise;
> Here in this pace from earth he took departure,
> Now he has got the garland of the martyr.
> Butchered by Clavers and his bloody band.
> Raging most ravenously o'er all the land,
> Only for owning Christ's supremacy,
> Wickedly wronged by encroaching tyranny.
> Nothing how near soever he to good
> Esteemed, nor dear for any truth his blood.

The Shining Light

And at the brightness of that light, which was before his eye,
His thick clouds pass'd away, hailstones and coals of fire did fly.
The Lord God also in the heav'ns did thunder in his ire;
And there the Highest gave his voice, hailstones and coals of fire.

Ye, he his arrows sent abroad, and them he scattered;
His lightnings also he shot out, and them discomforted.
The waters' channels then were seen, the world's foundations vast
At thy rebuke discover'd were, and at thy nostrils blast.

And from above the Lord sent down, and took me from below;
From many waters he me drew, which would me overflow.
He reliev'd from my strong foes, and such as did me hate;
Because he saw that they for me too strong were, and too great.

They me prevented in the day of my calamity;
But even then the Lord himself a stay was unto me.
He to a place where liberty and room was hath me brought;
Because he took delight in me, he my deliv'rance wrought.[1]

---

[1] The Comprehensive Psalter, Blue Banner Books, Rowlett, Texas, 2000, Psalm 18:12-19, pages 28-29.

John Nisbet
"I Think Well of Christ"

John Nisbet was born in 1627. He was a descendant of Murdoch Nisbet in Hardhill. Murdoch, a member of the Lollards, fled over seas because of the persecution. He brought with him a written copy of the New Testament which he constantly read and studied. John Nisbet came to love these Scriptures and the Christ of whom they spoke. John Nisbet was a strong, well-built man, who joined the army and spent some time in foreign countries. When he returned to Scotland, he swore the Covenants, as did King Charles at his coronation.

John married Margaret Law who proved to be a faithful solder of Christ as well as a wife who encouraged her husband in his fight against the armies of the king. They settle down for a while to a comfortable life until 1661 when King Charles and his counterfeit Protestants denied the principles of the Reformation. The Killing Time came with the king's army wanting to devour the Presbyterians of Scotland. John fought bravely in the battles. In the battle of Pentland Hills, November of 1679, John was severely wounded. He was stripped and his body was cast with the dead. But the Lord healed him. He felt that his suffering was given that he might preserve himself for the free enjoyment of the gospel, and to faithfully preach Christ in the fields. And so he did.

Margaret contended, with much grace, the afflictions and persecution, as one battle followed another. For four years Margaret bravely faced the steel of the enemy, along with her children. Sickness overtook her and she lay for eight days with her children beside her. Then she fell asleep in Jesus. It was in December of 1683 that she died "in a sheep's cot, where no light nor fire but that of a candle, no bed but that of straw, no stool but the ground to sit on."

John heard of his wife's death and returned to find her already buried. He also found a newly made coffin in which his daughter was laid. He saw his sons in a corner with fever, unable to hear his words. As he looked about him, his eyes were upon Christ. He testified, saying, "Naked come I into the world, and naked must I go out of it. The Lord is making my passage easy." His submission was not to the world but to the will of God. For two years John hid from the enemies of Christ. He wrote his "Large Testimony to Truth," wanting to preserve a witness to the gospel that would be there after he died. Meanwhile, a large price was placed on his head.

There came a time when John and three others were about the gospel and prayer. His son, James, spoke of this incident, saying, "it pleased God they were seen." Forty of the king's dragoons came upon them.

They set the house on fire. The four men came out and fought a lively fight. The leader of the dragoons was Captain Robert Nisbet. A redcoat and a relation to John, Captain Nisbet saw John as a rich prize, as money to line his pocket. This enemy of the King of kings killed John's fellow Covenanters in front of him, asking what he now thought of his circumstances. John Nisbet's reply was, "I think well of Christ and His cause as ever, and not at all the worse for what I suffer. Only I grieve and think myself at a loss that I am left in time when my three brethren are gone to heaven, whom you have wickedly murdered." Truly John was counted worthy to suffer for the sake of Christ. John Nisbet was tried quickly before the council and sentenced to death. Cruelly treated in prison he was unable to move because of the heavy chains and his terrible wounds. In this suffering he testified to the comfort of the Holy Spirit, "It pleased Him to give such real impression of unspeakable glory as without constant and immediate supports from the Giver will certainly overwhelm me."

As John came to the scaffold, he cried out: "My soul doth magnify the Lord; my soul doth magnify the Lord. I have longed these sixteen years to seal the precious cause and interest of the precious Christ with my blood, who hath answered and granted my request, and has left me no more to do but to come here and pour out my last prayer, sing forth my last praises of Him in time on this sweet and desirable scaffold, mount that ladder, and then I shall get home to my Father's house, see, enjoy, serve, and sing forth the praises of my glorious Redeemer for ever, world without end."

John committed his life to Christ on earth. He committed his soul to his heavenly Father on the scaffold. He left this life for heaven with the singing of the first six verses of Psalm 34, which begins, "God will I bless all times: His praise my mouth shall still express."

It was in the latter part of the 1600's that the faith of the church and the 'Scots Worthies' were tested in Scotland. It was what was called the "Killing times." King Charles had broken the covenant with the Presbyterians and Scotland. War was fought on the moor and mountains in the southern part of Scotland. These Presbyterians were called Covenanters, men and women, who carried the banner of Christ the King.

John Livingstone
His passion was Christ, and He alone

The first desire of John Livingstone was in the study of medicine. However, after spending a day in solitary with God on the banks of Mouse Water, he was moved to preach Christ. From that time on Livingstone had "one passion, and it was He, He alone." John Livingstone was born at Kilsyth in 1603. His father, William Livingstone, was a minister who was "straight and zealous in the work of the reformation." John was taught by his father to read and write, and was later sent to a Latin school at Stirling. In October of 1621 he received his degree from the College of Glasgow.

Livingstone, from the beginning of his ministry, met with the persecution of the times. For five years the Bishops prevented him from accepting calls from different churches. However, this didn't hinder his tongue from preaching the Word of his Savior. His ministry proved that the preaching of the Covenanters was other than cold and hard. His words of preaching had the flame of the Holy Spirit, captivating the souls of men for Christ. Livingstone was an architect of his sermons, an ambassador who took seriously his Master's word; "if my heart was lifted up, it was in preaching of Jesus Christ."

Livingstone preaching at the Kirk of Shotts.

On the twenty-first of June 1630, a revival broke out at the Kirk of Shotts. It was on a midsummer morning that Livingstone, wanting a respite from his responsibilities, went to the fields alone. He felt a burden of unworthiness, along with the great expectations of the people, to be of such a matter that he wished to escape. Yet his heart would not want to distrust God. He went to his preaching, ministering to the people from the Word. For an hour he preached from the text, "Then will I sprinkle clean water upon you, and ye shall be clean." Constrained by the Lord Himself, Livingstone continued on: "I was led on about an hour's time in a strain of exhortation and warning, with such liberty and melting of heart as I never had the like in publick all my life." Some 500 men and women, rich and poor alike could trace the "dawn of the undying life" to Livingstone's preaching that day.

John Livingstone's first parish was in Ireland, Killenchy in the County of Down. In 1638 this worthy Scot again crossed the channel to

Stranraer, where he spent ten years, followed by fourteen summers in Ancrum. This ministry was followed by his ejection from Scotland by the Privy Council. In Ireland John Livingstone and others were so harassed by the church Bishops that they decided to build a ship near Belfast. The ship would be of 150 ton burden and called, the Eagle Wing. In 1636 they were of mind to sail for New England of the Pilgrim Fathers. It was not to be. As they sailed toward the new land storms were raised to such velocity that they felt it was the hand of the Lord leading them back. They returned to Ulster. While on board, a baby boy was born to Mr. and Mrs. Michael Coltheard. Livingstone baptized the boy, naming him Seaborn.

John Livingstone was a man of great humility and modesty. He said of those other faithful ministers of the Word, "Every minister of my acquaintance gets his work done better than I; yet I would not desire to be another than myself, nor to have other manner than the Lord uses, for His power is made perfect in weakness." Livingstone, though humble in his ministry for Christ, was a scholar. He was fluent in Hebrew and Chaldee, reading the Bible in Spanish and German, and acquainted with French, Italian, and Dutch.

His household was filled with love. He married the eldest daughter of Bartholomew Fleming, a merchant of Edinburgh. He was married to Janet in the year 1635. She was a most worthy wife. Years after Livingstone died, the clouds of persecution hung even lower over Presbyterian Scotland. Janet Livingstone faced the Earl of Rothes, and other enemies of Christ, seeking the liberty of those ill-treated ministers of the Master.

In 1660 Charles II was restored to the throne and Livingstone knew that the persecution would weigh heavily upon Scotland. In 1662 Parliament and Council had, by proclamation, sought to remove all Presbyterian ministers who had come since 1649. At the last communion which Livingstone had at Ancrum, in October, after the sermon on Monday, it pleased the Lord to open his mouth, encouraging his listeners in their suffering in the present controversy of the Kingdom of Christ.

In December Livingstone was called before the Council at Edinburgh, asking him to take an oath of allegiance. This he could not do. He had 48 hours to leave Edinburgh. He traveled to Leith, and from there in 1663, he left to preach to the Scots at Rotterdam. The following December his wife and two of their children came to him. In his last few years Livingstone found difficulty in walking because of an illness. He died in Rotterdam on August 9, 1672. Some of his last words were, "Carry my commendation to Jesus Christ, till I come thee myself."

Mrs. John Livingstone
Choice Mrs. Livingstone, a mother indeed in Israel

Janet Fleming, eldest daughter of Bartholomew, a merchant in Edinburgh, was married to John Livingstone on June 23, 1635. They were married by John's father in the West Church of Edinburgh. Janet Livingstone stayed beside her husband through many trials as he faithfully preached the gospel of Christ, both in Ireland and Scotland. John was banished to Holland, Janet following him, with two of their children, that same year. She remained with her husband until his death in August of 1672.

Janet Livingstone returned to Scotland, living in Edinburgh. She and other ladies of the Covenant (Presbyterian) helped the nonconforming ministers, praying for their liberty in the preaching of God's Word. Mrs. Livingstone, and other ladies, drew up a petition which they presented to the council, bringing upon themselves the hatred of the government, archbishops and bishops. However, they honored their Savior.

In the early part of 1674 a cessation from persecution took place, called "the Blink." Fearing that this peace would be short lived, the ministers of Christ preached with more zeal than before, both in the houses and in the fields. This "Blink" was short and of political nature. Two parties of the government sought power, each one blaming the other for allowing preaching in the fields by these "seminaries of rebellion." Persecution rose again in Scotland under the leadership of Lauderdale, who secretly encouraged the conventicles, and then blamed the opposition for allowing them to continue. The pulpits of the ministers were once again invaded as the militia sought out the ringleaders of the preaching fields.

Mrs. Livingstone and others, especially wives and widows of the ousted ministers, including those of high rank, prayed fervently, and petitioned the council on behalf of the ministers of the Word. They drew up a petition and chose Janet Livingstone to present it to the Lord Chancellor, Earl of Rothes. Fourteen other ladies were to present copies to the principal chancellors. The day came, June 4, and the Chancellor's coach came first. Archbishop Sharp was also on that coach. Mrs. Livingstone stepped out to hand the petition to the Chancellor

Mrs. Livingstone presenting the Petition to Lord-Chancellor Rothes.

while the crowd of ladies pressed on behind her. The scene brought fear to the heart of Sharp and he hid behind the Chancellor. And so he should fear. For he was the one who persecuted many Presbyterians, and the ladies whom he called, "the fanatic wives of Edinburgh."

However, they came only to present their petition. The petition which Mrs. Livingstone presented to the Chancellor read in part: "May it therefore please your lordships to grant such liberty to our honest ministers, . . . that we may, to the comfort of our souls, enjoy the rich blessing of faithful pastors, and that our pastors may be delivered from any sinful compliance with what is contrary to the known judgment of honest Presbyterians."

On June 11, about a dozen names were gathered and called before the council. The ladies' defense was that they were starving through want of the gospel. They were told to go peaceably to their homes. However, the council intended to have their homes raided, to surprise them and place them in prison. They heard of their plans and escaped. Throughout the year the council sought to persecute the ladies. On June 25 some ladies refused an invitation to come before the council. They soon found themselves in prison. The London court urged the council to deal harshly with the ladies, his majesty requiring them to use their "utmost rigor in finding out and bringing to just judgment the ringleaders . . . "

Mrs. Livingstone was discovered as the one who presented the petition to the chancellor. She was charged with "seditious and unlawful practices." Her name stands among other worthy ladies, such as Mrs. Elizabeth Rutherford, Rachel Aird, and Catherine (widow of Robert Blair). Mrs. Rutherford, and others who were his majesty's rebels were put to the horn, and their possessions gathered for his highness' use. Letters kept coming from the council about these seditious and wicked persons, enemies of his majesty, who should be punished. As with their husbands and other faithful pastors, the ladies of the Covenant held fast to their true King and Savior, Jesus Christ. The true enemies were those who sought the life of those who were faithful to the King of kings.

On the twelfth of November Mrs. Livingstone was banished from the city of Edinburgh. After a short absence she and other ladies returned to their homes in Edinburgh. They continued to be an offense to the government. Janet Livingstone went back to Holland. Friends lovingly wrote of her in letters to one another. She found honor in such thoughts as, "I salute much in the Lord that mother in Israel, choice Mrs. Livingstone, and her sweet daughter." In covenant with their Lord, the ladies stood beside the preachers of the gospel, ever ready to face prison for the cause of Christ.

Lady Colvill
So Zealous A Covenanter

Margaret Wemyss married Robert, the second Lord Colvill of Ochiltree. As Lady Colvill she bore one son and two daughters. Robert died in 1671. Their son Robert became the third Lord Colvill.

Lady Colvill was treated severely by the government for she steadfastly held to her faith in Christ as her Savior, and to the persecuted cause of the Presbyterians. She was classed with the "desperate and implacable party who keep seditious and numerous field conventicles, and that in open contempt of our authority, as if it were to brave us and those that are in places of trust under us." During these "killing times" this was a "badge of honorable distinction."

It was Archbishop Sharp who gave her the honor of being counted among the Ladies of the Covenant against whom the government showed their wrath. For he endeavored to arrest and put down the progress of these "fanaticism Ladies." Lady Colvill was faithful in attending the open field meetings, hearing the best of the ministers of the word, including Samuel Arnot and Thomas Hog of Larbert. She befriended these ministers of our Lord, giving them lodging and food in her home.

Such was the persecution in Scotland that soldiers were sent to disperse the people as they gathered in the fields. On one such occasion they scattered the people with no resistance. However, the Archbishop told the council that they resisted fiercely, and many were summoned to appear before the council at Edinburgh. Lady Colvill's name was on the list. She and others were summoned to appear on July 9, 1674. It was prudent that she disobey the summons, dreading immediate imprisonment upon appearing. These ladies were denounced as his majesty's rebels.

Lady Colvill was called again to appear before the council on September 15. Again she did not appear and was fined. The council issued letters against her and about 100 others. Many of these women were of high station. Sheriffs and their deputies, magistrates and others, were sent to capture these Covenanters and commit them to prison.

By the year 1677 public meetings were being held at night because of the fury of the king's army, some meetings being held in the house of Lady Colvill. She and her friends lay under a sentence of jail until the king's proclamation of June 29, 1679 suspended the letters. Lady Colvill, at all times, faithfully and zealously attended the preaching of God's Word in the fields, entertaining in her house the "nonconforming" ministers of the King of kings. Both she and many of her household were hunted through the years for their faithfulness to Christ.

A captain Carstairs was sent out by Archbishop Sharp under false pretenses, and, coming to the home of Lady Colvill on a Sabbath day with about a dozen soldiers, proceeded to capture Robert Anderson who was preaching, among others. Having allowed a Robert Steedman to escape the captain went into a fit of a convulsion for about two hours. So the Lord gave Lady Colvill and her young son, Robert, time to escape. Lady Colvill loved the Word of God and so gave her son a sound education in the doctrines of Christ, and in the principles of Presbytery and Covenant. She taught those things which she judged to be founded upon the Word of God, and connected with the honor of her Lord and Savior.

However, the Privy Council was intent on taking her son from her. For, like other tyrannical systems, they sought to deliver Scotland from the Presbyterians by going after their children, to take them from their parents. As early as 1662 Parliament had decreed that the masters and professors of Universities, etc., should be licensed by the bishop of the diocese, and pledge allegiance to the church of the archbishops. Lady Colvill had no intention of allowing her son to be taken from her, to be taught what was contrary to God's Word. She took him away. The government proceeded against her by fining her, and soon she was thrown into prison on December 2, 1684 in Edinburgh. Charges against her were for bringing up her son in fanaticism and other disloyal principles, delivering him from the council and committing him to the education of others.

 Lady Colvill's prison was dark and narrow, having to burn a candle throughout the day. Neither was there a fire to take away the dampness of the winter days. The faithful in Scotland knew that Lady Colvill was there because she did not countenance the profane clergy of that day. Robert, Lord Colvill, was attending the college of Edinburgh while his mother was in prison. She was a worthy servant of Christ, never seeking to gain freedom from prison by denying her Lord or her faith. She was allowed to leave the prison for a while because of her illness. And, under a bond of payment, she was allowed to leave to help her son. Whether she returned to prison we do not know, but orders were given to apprehend her, and to see her re-entered into the prison of Edinburgh.

It was written of Lady Colvill that she was entitled to that benediction of the Savior, "Rejoice, and be exceeding glad; for great is your reward in heaven, for so persecuted they the prophets which were before you."

George Wishart
Offered his life for Christ

On May 28, 1546, Cardinal Beaton opened the door of the castle and sought deliverance by claiming, "I am a priest, I am a priest." Norma and John Leslie, William Kircaldy, James Melville, and Peter Carmichael had come to the castle to avenge the killing of George Wishart. The Cardinal was stabbed two or three times by Melville. They then held the Castle of St. Andrews for two years until the French secured the Castle, and the safety of these followers of the Lord. The tension between the faithful preachers of the Gospel and the enemy of the Word is something that few of us understand today. However, the faithfulness of George Wishart urges us to be faithful in the face of persecution.

From the very beginning of Wishart's ministry he felt the breath of the enemy. He was educated at the University of Cambridge and was known for both his eloquence of speech and agreeable manner. He began his teaching in 1544 in the town of Montrose. A fellow scholar wrote of George Wishart: "He was a man of tall stature, black-haired, long bearded, of graceful personage, eloquent, courteous, ready to teach, and desirous to learn." He frequently gave parts of the clothing he wore to the poor. From Montrose he went to Dundee where he acquired a reputation through his public discourses on the Epistle of Romans. Such was his teaching that the Romanist clergy began to feel that if he were allowed to go on, he would pull down the tapestry of superstition and idolatry, which they worked so hard to build. As with Paul  and the silversmiths, they were disgusted and alarmed at the reception Wishart met in Dundee.

In 1539 Cardinal Beaton succeeded to the See of St. Andrews. He carefully followed the path of his uncle. He gained the approval of Rome by accusing John Borthwick of heresy, confiscated his goods, and burnt him in effigy when he escaped out of the country. Cardinal Beaton himself ended up as a prisoner in the Castle of Dalkeith for forging the will of King James V, declaring himself to be one of the regents of the kingdom. Such were the times of persecution in Scotland. Cardinal Beaton soon escaped his imprisonment to carry on his war against the Scots Worthies, by shedding the blood of these saints. Several professors of the Reformed faith were imprisoned, condemned, hanged, drowned, or banished. This was the Cardinal who was incensed at George Wishart's success in Dundee. It was at the end of one of George's sermons that a charge was read against him that he would leave the town and trouble the people no longer. His reply was, in part, "God is my witness that I never minded your trouble, but your comfort . . . but sure I am, to reject the Word of God, and drive away His messengers, is not the way to save you from trouble, but to bring you into it . . ." He further pleaded with his enemies that they hear the Spirit of Truth and repent of their sins. From Dundee Wishart went to the West country.

Wherever Wishart went, he was faithful in the preaching of the Word of His Savior and King, Christ Jesus. Great numbers crowded around him as he preached, as in the town of Ayr. Again the thorn of Cardinal Beaton was thrust into his side. The Cardinal followed this troubler, if not in person, in influencing others to get rid of Wishart. Beaton urged the Archbishop of Glasgow to go to Ayr. There the Archbishop took possession of the church to prevent Wishart from preaching. However, you cannot stop the voice of God. It was the Archbishop who soon left town because of his attitude toward the people and his inability to give a good sermon.

One night the Sheriff of Ayr came and set up a garrison of soldiers in the church to keep out George Wishart. The people were willing to storm the church, willing to fight to have Wishart preach. However, Wishart encouraged them to follow him out to fields, telling them of how Christ preached by the sea and before the mountain. There in the fields the multitude heard the preaching of Christ's Gospel for more than three hours. Confession and tears came to many as the Spirit worked in their hearts.

There was the time when a plague broke out in Dundee. Wishart traveled to Dundee and soon was preaching at its East-gate. Those who were well gathered close to him, while those who were infected heard him from the back. His text was, "He sent his Word, and healed them, and delivered them from their destructions." Without reservation he comforted even the most infectious of the people. And he made sure that the poor were not wanting for their basic needs. This was the time when the Cardinal attempted to have Wishart assassinated.

Wishart offered his life for Christ, faithfully preaching the Word from city to city, from Inveresk to Edinburgh. When George Wishart came to the scaffold, he spoke to the people, saying, "I entreat you that you love the Word of God for your salvation, and suffer patiently and with a comfortable heart for the Word's sake, which is your everlasting comfort; but for the true Gospel, which was given me by the grace of God, I suffer this day with a glad heart." He was bound to the stake, which was ready for the fire, in March of 1546. Even with his body scorched he witnessed to the love of Christ.

James Stuart
A Nobleman in the court of the King of kings

James Stuart, Earl of Moray, was the natural son of King James V, brother to Mary Queen of Scots. He was placed early under the care of George Buchanan and became a principal agent in promoting the work of Reformation from Popery. In the year 1555 James attended the

preaching of John Knox at Calder where he often wished that his doctrine was made more public. James had a love and zeal for the doctrines of the Reformation.

In 1556 James and Argyle wrote to John Knox, who was in Geneva, to return to Scotland and further the Reformation. Knox committed his Geneva flock to John Calvin. However, it was not until the second of May 1559 that he arrived and first preached at Dundee, and then at Perth. It was

at this time that the Queen Regent was putting preachers to the horn, prohibiting others from giving them comfort or assistance upon pain of rebellion. This enraged the people and they would not be restrained from pulling down the images of idolatry. This so enraged the Queen that she caused her French army to march toward the town.

Hearing of the success of John Knox, the Queen Regent, Mary of Guise, sent Lord James (Earl of Moray) and the Earl of Argyle to ask the intent of the assembly. John Knox's reply was that she was to be told that "her enterprise will not succeed in the end; for she fights not against man only, but against the eternal God." The Queen summoned the preachers and noblemen to leave the town of St. Johnston. She promised that they could leave peaceably. However, she took possession of the town and put a French Garrison in it. This was a breach of promise that led the Earls of Argyle and Moray (James Stuart) to forsake her and join the Lords of the Congregations who favored the work of the Reformation.

There was great zeal in the gospel of these worthy noblemen of Scotland as they encouraged people to turn away from the superstition of Popery to the Reformed religion. So great was their purging of the relics of idolatry that the Queen Regent's zeal gave way to fears about her civil authority. The queen proclaimed that these men were in open rebellion against her, pretending that their real design was to set Lord James on the throne in her place. She produced a letter claiming that it came from Francis and Mary, King and Queen of France. This 'forged' letter was to James himself, upbraiding him for his rebellion, commanding him to lay down his arms. His answer declared his allegiance to the Regent and law.

He also stated that he and the nobles had undertaken the reformation of religion to the glory of God, and therefore were willing to bear reproach for the cause of Christ, as He alone is the Head and Defender of the faith. The Queen continued her attack against the noblemen of the court which distinguished them in promoting the faith of the Reformation. The Queen received letters from the Pope and uncles, the Guises of France, requesting her to put an end to the efforts of James. He later went to England and then to France. After the Queen was in custody in Lochleven, he returned to Scotland.

In the year 1567 James Stuart, Earl of Moray, was made Regent. James resolved to tour through the whole kingdom to settle the courts of justice and repair what was wrong. His adversaries, the Hamiltons, and even astrologers who told him he had little time to live, did not hinder his determination to see Scotland find peace. He summoned a Convention of Estates to meet at Glasgow to redress some grievances. Meanwhile, the Queen escaped from Lochleven Castle. James Stuart and his friends decided to remain in Glasgow. The Queen's army of 6500 strong

THE REGENT MORAY'S HOUSE, EDINBURGH.

traveled past Glasgow to lodge the Queen in Dumbarton Castle. The Regent was informed of their plans and was waiting with his noblemen and townspeople. The battle was fought on May 13, 1568. They obtained victory over the Queen's army and the Queen fled to England. James and his troops went back to Glasgow thanking God for their deliverance from those who threatened to overturn the work of God.

James' administration passed many salutary laws in favor of civil and religious liberty. This made him more and more the object of Popish malice. The enemy failed time and again to get rid of him. He was mortally wounded by a bullet which entered a little below the navel, killing the horse of George Douglas behind him. He began to settle his affairs leaving the young King in care of his noble friends. Without a reproachful word James died on January 23, 1570.

Buchanan wrote that his death was "lamented by all good men, who loved him as the public father of his country." Though he was valiant in war, James desired peace and showed much mercy and justice to the poor. James Stuart had married a daughter of the Earl of March. His home "was like a holy temple; after meals he caused a chapter of the Bible to be read, and asked the opinions of learned men as were present on it." He had both a desire to learn and to practice what was in the Scriptures. Another wrote of James Stuart: "A man truly good, and worthy to be ranked amongst the best governors that this kingdom hath enjoyed, and therefore to this day honored with the title of The Good Regent" (Spottiswoode).

How doth Christ execute the office of a king?[1]

Christ executeth the office of a king, in subduing us to himself, in ruling and defending us, and in restraining and conquering all his and our enemies.

Christ's Kingly Office

Jesus Christ is of mighty renown, he is a king; (1.) he has a kingly title, 'High and Lofty' Isa lvii 15. (2.) He has his *insignia regalia*, his ensigns of royalty; *corona est insigne regae potestatis* [a crown symbol of royal power]. He has his crown, Rev vi 2; his sword, 'Gird thy sword upon thy thigh' Psa xlv 3; his sceptre, 'A sceptre of righteousness is the sceptre of thy kingdom' Heb I 8. (3.) He has his *excutcheon*, or coat of armour; he inserts the lion in his coat of arms, 'The lion of the tribe of Judah' Rev v 5. The text says 'he is King of kings.' He has a pre-eminence of all other kings, and is called, 'The Prince of the kings of the earth' Rev I 5. He must needs be so, for 'by him kings reign' Prov viii 15. They hold their crowns by immediate tenure from this great King. Christ infinitely outlives all other princes; he has the highest throne, the largest dominions, and the longest possession, 'Thy throne, O God, is for ever and ever' Heb i 8. He has many heirs, but no successors. Well may he be called 'King of kings,' for he has an unlimited power. The power of other kings is limited, but Christ's power is unlimited. 'Whatsoever he pleased, that did he, in heaven and earth, and in the seas' Psa cxxxv 6. Christ's power is as large as his will. The angels take the oath of allegiance to him. 'Let all the angels of God worship him' Heb i 6.

–Thomas Watson[2]

---

[1] The Westminster Catechism, ibid, The Shorter Catechism Q&A 26, pages 293-294.
[2] A Body of Divinity, Thomas Watson, The Banner of Truth Trust, London, 1970, page 187.

Psalm LIV[1]

Save me, O God, by thy great name,
And judge me by thy strength;
Hear thou my prayer, O God; give ear
Unto my words at length.
For they that strangers are to me
Do up against me rise;
Oppressors seek my soul, and God
Set not before their eyes

Lo, God an helper is to me,
And therefore I am bold;
The Lord hath taken part with those
That do my soul uphold.
Unto my foes their wickedness
He surely shall repay;
O for thy truth's sake cut them off,
And sweep them clean away.

I with a willing mind will give
A sacrifice to thee;
Thy name, O Lord, because 'tis good,
Shall be extolled by me.
Because he hath delivered me
From all adversities;
And its desire mine eye hath seen
Upon mine enemies.

---

[1] The Psalter, A Revised Edition of the Scottish Metrical Version of the Psalms, Blackie & Son, Dublin, 1881, page 104; "…to make it a more faithful conveyance of the original and a more suitable vehicle of the Church's praise."

James Guthrie
'Mr. Sickerfoot'

James Guthrie first met Christ while he was professor of philosophy at St. Andrews. His soul was awakened through the friendship of Samuel Rutherford and the weekly prayer meetings with teachers and students, where "Christ was in the midst, their friend." Before he died, James testified before the Parliament that "until the year 1638, I was treading other steps; and the Lord did then graciously recover me out of the snare of Prelacy, Ceremonies and the Service Book."

Before Guthrie was ordained, he signed the National Covenant. On  his way to the signing he passed the town's hangman, which made him "walk up and down a little before he went forward." With this vision of death he wrote his autograph to the Covenant. James Guthrie was a Scots Worthy minister of the gospel for twenty-two years. He ministered to the souls of Lauder and Stirling. James Cowie, his precentor, servant, and friend, said of him that he kept his personal religion as if he "had been a young convert." The manse at Stirling was called, "a little church of God."

Once when James lay near death his attendant was told to read the ninth chapter of Romans. As the words, "I will have mercy on whom I will have mercy," were read, he broke into tears. His testimony was that he had no sentence to lean upon as this pronouncement of Sovereignty and love. Soon after, through the prayers of friends, he regained his health.

It was the Malignants of Stirling who gave Mr. Guthrie the name of "Sickerfoot." This man of God was sure of foot, "steadfast, unmovable, always abounding in the work of the Lord." Oliver Cromwell spoke of him as "That short man who could not bow." James Guthrie would rather die "a violent death for Christ and His cause," than rest upon a sick bed to have his senses dulled. If he had to go to the scaffold for Christ's sake, it would be to step "into eternity with the utmost distinctness and in the immediate exercise of prayer and faith."

James Sharp was a promising young student while Guthrie was regent at St. Andrews. Some years later, August of the Restoration year, Guthrie and others drew up an address to the king. They prayed for His Majesty, and besought him to conserve the Reformed faith, and keep the Covenants to which he had sworn. They called upon the king to be like a David, a man after God's own heart, or a Josias who humbled himself before God. Any land would be blessed with such leaders who humbled themselves before Christ the King. But Charles did not desire a theocracy. And before many hours passed, ten preachers and two laymen were made prisoners of Edinburgh Castle. It was Archbishop Sharp who zealously came after the Covenanters, hating the wholehearted Protester, James Guthrie, eager to punish the man who once had him excommunicated.

James Guthrie was never to be free again. The indictment against him included the book he authored, "The Causes of the Lord's Wrath Against Scotland." This book was honored along sides that of Samuel Rutherford's, "Lex Rex." It was held as treason for anyone to own either of them. James Guthrie stood strong before the "Drunken Parliament" in 1661, saying, "My Lord, my conscience I cannot submit; but this old crazy body and mortal flesh I do submit, to do with it whatsoever you will, whether by death or banishment or imprisonment or anything else . . . (it) will not extinguish the Covenant or work of the Reformation since 1638."

The first of June came when he was to be hung at the Cross. His faithful friend and servant, James Cowie, was with him to the end, seeing the majesty of God in his master, "God's glory smote him on the face." "Sure of Foot" did not falter as he came to the steps of the scaffold, saying, "I durst not redeem my life with the loss of my integrity, I did judge it better to suffer than to sin." Also, "Art Thou from everlasting, O Lord my God. I shall not die but live." His last words were, as he lifted the cloth from his face, "The Covenants, The Covenants shall yet be Scotland's reviving."

His wife and daughter, Sophia, were banished from Scotland. James Guthrie was hung, his head cut off to be placed on an arch between High Street and the Canongate. James Cowie held Guthrie's son, William, from seeing his father hung, but he could not stop him from seeing his father's head being bleached by the sun, year after year, a heavy weight upon a Covenanter's child. William did grow up to honor Christ Jesus and the Covenants, but died young. His father's head hung above Netherport of Edinburgh for 27 years, until a Sandie Hamilton, a lover of the gospel and student for the Covenanting minister, climbed the Post, at risk of his life, took down the skull and reverently buried it.

Another great Scots Worthy was William Guthrie, his cousin. He could not attend the death of James because of sickness and the fear of being imprisoned himself. He died a few years later. He was a student of Samuel Rutherford. William was considered one of the great preachers of Scotland, thousands coming to Christ. His ministry is still with us today, in his book, "The Christian's Great Interest."

"The Covenants, The Covenants shall yet be Scotland's reviving."

In THE COVENANTER of 1858,[1] the headline read THE REVIVAL OF THE SOLEMN LEAGUE AND COVENANT. The article commented on James Guthrie's comment, "The Covenants, The Covenants shall yet be Scotland's reviving." We need, especially as those of the Reformed Body, need to take a good look at this Covenant, that we may revive our understanding of Christ and His Kingdom, especially in relations to the nations, all of whom must honor the Son. The beginning paragraphs of the article draws us to such a Christ:

"The prophetic last words of the martyr Guthrie are familiar to all who love the principles of a faithful testimony against Antichrist, and have a due regard to the Scriptural vows of the nation—'The Covenants—the Covenants will yet be the reviving of Scotland.' The God of Zion, we are assured, ever remembers his Covenant. The glory of the Mediator—the supreme authority of His word—the peace, purity, and liberty of His church—and the prosperity and blessing of nations, are all concerned in maintaining firmly the descending obligation of Covenants which are moral in their nature, and which were entered into with Divine approval.

Such, beyond any doubt, is the character of the Solemn League and Covenant; and there is the most ample and satisfactory evidence that at the time it was framed and taken, it was eminently owned of God, as an instrument for advancing His glory—and that it has been acknowledged on many occasions since, as a means of preserving the truth, and of promoting the cause of pure and undefiled religion. When this justly celebrated Bond was brought in, on the suggestion of the excellent Alexander Henderson—adopted by the General Assembly of the Church of Scotland, in 1643—and joyfully taken and sworn by the Westminster Assembly, the two Houses of the British Parliament, and by all classes throughout these kingdoms—it effectually arrested the progress of great evils—formed a defense against the machinations and power of numerous enemies—united the friends of truth in firm concord—and achieved, to a great extent, the Scriptural liberties of the nation. To this admirable League we are mainly indebted for our Westminster Standards; and had not evil times and evil men arrested the progress of the great reformation which it inaugurated, not only had the churches in Britain been brought to a happy uniformity, but the whole policy of Britain had likewise been conformed to a Scriptural model; and other European nations and churches had, according to the noble design of Henderson,

---

[1] The Covenanter, Vol. II, Belfast, 1858, page 257.

been united in a sacred bond of brotherhood, for promoting the great interests of genuine Protestantism, and the universal establishment of Christ's Kingdom.

The Westminster Assembly and the Covenant of 1643

The Assembly of representatives from various understandings of church polity met, by *"An ordinance of the Lords and Commons,"* at Westminster, in the "King Henry the VII's Chapel," July 1, 1643. Every member who was admitted to sit in the Assembly took this *Promise and Vow.* "I ___ do seriously promise and vow, in the presence of Almighty God, That in this Assembly, whereof I am a member, I will maintain nothing in point of doctrine, but what I believe to be most agreeable to the word of God; not in point of discipline, but what may make most for God's glory, and the peace and good of this church."[1]

The Scots commissioners, appointed by the General Assembly of the Church of Scotland, were present at the Assembly, not by appointment, but by virtue of an invitation from both Houses of Parliament and from the Assembly; "conveyed to them by the commissioners sent down by these respective bodies to solicit aid from the Church of Scotland, and also in virtue of the authority of the General Assembly, by which, in compliance with this call, they had been delegated."[2] Included in the commissioners from the General Assembly of the Church of Scotland were the Ministers, Alexander Henderson of Edinburgh, Robert Douglas of Edinburgh Samuel Rutherford of St. Andrews, Robert Baillie of Glasgow, and George Gillespie of Edinburgh. These names remind us of the "Killing Times of 1685," which was soon to be felt by the faithful preachers of the Gospel.

Upon the arrival of the Scots commissioners, about ten days after the beginning of the Assembly, a discussion of the Covenant of 1643 was brought to the floor. The Solemn League and was discussed, clause by clause, for several days. "With some slight alterations, it was solemnly taken by the House of Commons and the Assembly of divine; and soon after by the House of Lords and the congregations in and about London. The circumstances exerted a powerful influence over the deliberations of the Westminster Assembly. The league had for its object, not merely to secure 'the preservation of the reformed religion of the Church of Scotland;' but 'the reformation of religion in the kingdoms of England and Ireland, in doctrine, worship, discipline, and government, according

[1] Westminster Confession of Faith, Free Presbyterian Publications, Glasgow, 2001, page 15.
[2] Historical Sketch of The Westminster Assembly of Divines, William Symington, Presbyterian's Armoury Publications, Australia, 2002, page 17.

to the word of God, and the example of the best reformed churches; and to bring the churches of God in the three kingdoms o the nearest conjunction and uniformity in religion, Confession of Faith, Form of Church Government, Directory for Worship, and Catechizing (Article I).'" Dr. Symington then makes this observation that it "appears that the objects proposed by the Westminster Assembly and by the Solemn League were thus far identical, while the latter served only more clearly to define the intention of the former. The Assembly, therefore, set itself to the task of framing a basis of covenanted uniformity in Doctrine, Discipline, Worship, and Government, for the three kingdoms."[1]

To put it in the vernacular of today, this is when 'the rubber hits the road.' It is one thing to catch the ball, and another thing to claim it for your own and run with it. The persecution "unto death" does not come to those on the side-line, but to those who run the race. The Westminster Confession and the Solemn League and Covenant, both understand that the Scriptures are to be rule of practice for the God-established institutions of Family, Church, and Government. As Christ is the King of kings, He rules over each of these institutions. Though it is not a church institution that is to control the civil government, nor are the appointed magistrates and princes to have authority over the Savior's Church; but all governments are instated by the Creator and are to be ruled by His divine Scriptures.

Thus, when Christ and His righteousness reigns and His moral Law and precepts are obeyed, then blessings flow to all people. Also, because of the wickedness of man, when the Lord's faithful followers desire righteousness in Doctrine, Discipline, Worship, and Government; then there will be tribulation and persecution. Christians seek to obey the Word of God in church, family, and civil governments. Civil disobedience comes only at the point when Christians face the question as to obey the Triune God or the creature who desires transgression rather than righteousness. 'Be like us' the wicked cry, and 'we will give you life.' To be like Christ is our way of life, ransomed souls whose eternal inheritance is promised and received. For in Christ "we have obtained an inheritance, being predestinated according to the purpose of him who worketh all things after the counsel of his own will; that we should be to the praise of his glory, who first trusted in Christ. In whom ye also trusted, after that ye believed, ye were sealed with that Holy Spirit of promise, which is the earnest of our inheritance until the redemption of the purchased possession, unto the praise of his glory" (Eph. 1:11-14).

---

[1] Ibid, page 26.

Concerning the Observation of Days of Public Thanksgiving

When any such day is to be kept, let notice be given of it, and of the occasion thereof, some convenient time before, that the people may the better prepare themselves thereunto.

The day being come, and the congregation (after private preparations) being assembled, the minister is to begin with a word of exhortation, to stir up the people to the duty for which they are met, and with a short prayer for God's assistance and blessing, (as at other conventions for publick worship,) according to the particular occasion of their meeting.

Let him then make some pithy narration of the deliverance obtained, or mercy received, or of whatever hath occasioned that assembling of the congregation, that all may better understand it, and more affected with it.

And, because the singing of psalms is of all other the most proper ordinance for expressing of joy and thanksgiving, let some pertinent psalm or psalms be sung for that purpose, before or after the reading of some portion of the word suitable to the present business.

Then let the minister, who is to preach, proceed to further exhortation and prayer before his sermon, with special reference to the present work: after which, let him preach upon some text of Scripture pertinent to the occasion.[1]

Of Singing of Psalms

It is the duty of Christians to praise God publickly, by singing of psalms together in the congregation, and also privately in the family.

In singing of psalms, the voice is to be tunably and gravely ordered; but the chief care must be to sing with understanding, and with grace in the heart, making melody unto the Lord.

That the whole congregation may join therein, every one that can read is to have psalm book; and all others, not disabled by age or otherwise, are to be exhorted to learn to read. But for the present, where many in the congregation cannot read, it is convenient that the minister, or some other fit person appointed by him and the other ruling officers, do read the psalm, line by line, before the singing thereof.[2]

---

[1] Westminster Confession of Faith, ibid, The Directory for THE PUBLICK WORSHIP OF GOD; AGREED UPON BY THE ASSEMBLY OF DIVINES AT WESTMINSTER WITH THE ASSISTANCE OF COMMISSIONERS FROM THE CHURCH OF SCOTLAND, AS A PART OF THE COVENANTED UNIFORMITY IN RELIGION BETWIXT THE CHURCHES OF CHRIST IN THE KINGDOMS OF SCOTLAND, ENGLAND, AND IRELAND, pages 392-393.

[2] Ibid, page 393.

The Solemn League and Covenant, 1643[1]

We Noblemen, Barons, Knights, Gentlemen, Citizens, Burgesses, Ministers of the Gospel, and Commons of all sorts, in the kingdoms of Scotland, England, and Ireland, by the providence of GOD, living under one King, and being of one reformed religion, having before our eyes the glory of GOD, and the advancement of the kingdom of our Lord and Saviour JESUS CHRIST, the honour and happiness of the King's majesty and his posterity, and the true publick liberty, safety, and peace of the kingdoms, wherein every one's private condition is included: And calling to mind the treacherous and bloody plots, conspiracies, attempts, and especially in these three kingdoms, ever since the reformation of religion; and how much their rage, power, and presumption are of late, and at this time, increased and exercised, whereof the deplorable state of the church and kingdom of Ireland, the distressed estate of the church and kingdom of England, and the dangerous estate of the church and kingdom of Scotland, are present and public testimonies; we have now at last (after other means of supplication, remonstrance, protestation, and suffering,) for the preservation of ourselves and our religion from utter ruin and destruction, according to the commendable practice of these kingdoms in former times, and the example of GOD'S people in other nations, after mature deliberation, resolved and determined to enter into a mutual and Solemn League and Covenant, wherein we all subscribe, and each one of us for himself, with our hands lifted up to the most High GOD, do swear,

I. That we shall sincerely, really, and constantly, through the grace of GOD, endeavour, in our several places and callings, the preservation of the reformed religion in the Church of Scotland, in doctrine, worship, discipline, and government, against our common enemies; the reformation of religion in the kingdoms of England and Ireland, in doctrine, worship, discipline, and government, according to the Word of GOD, and the example of the best reformed Churches; and shall endeavour to bring the Churches of GOD in the three kingdoms to the nearest conjunction and uniformity in religion, confession of faith, form of church-government, directory for worship and catechizing; that we, and our posterity after us, may, as brethren, live in faith and love, and the Lord may delight to dwell in the midst of us.

II. That we shall in like manner, without respect of persons, endeavour the extirpation of Popery, Prelacy, (that is, church government

---

[1] Westminster Confession of Faith, Ibid, THE SOLEMN LEAGUE AND COVENANT, pages 358-360.

by Archbishops, Bishops, their Chancellors, and Commissaries, Deans, Deans and Chapters, Archdeacons, and all other ecclesiastical officers depending on that hierarchy,) superstition, heresy, schism, profaneness, and whatsoever shall be found contrary to sound doctrine and the power of godliness; lest we partake in other men's sins, and thereby be in danger to receive of their plagues; and that the Lord may be one, and his name one, in the three kingdoms.

III. We shall, with the same sincerity, reality, and constancy, in our several vocations, endeavour, with our estates and lives, mutually to preserve the rights and privileges of the Parliaments, the liberties of the kingdoms; and to preserve and defend the King's Majesty's person and authority, in the preservation and defense of the true religion, and liberties of the kingdoms; that the world may bear witness with our consciences of our loyalty, and that we have no thoughts or intentions to diminish his Majesty's just power and greatness.

IV. We shall also, with all faithfulness, endeavour the discovery of all such as have been or shall be incendiaries, malignants, or evil instruments, by hindering the reformation of religion, dividing the king from his people, or one of the kingdoms from another, or making any faction or parties amongst the people, contrary to this League and Covenant; that they may be brought to publick trial, and receive condign punishment, as the degree of their offences shall require or deserve, or the supreme judicatories of both kingdoms respectively, or others having power from them for that effect, shall judge convenient.

V. And whereas the happiness of a blessed peace between these kingdoms, denied in former times to our progenitors, is, by the good providence of GOD, granted unto us, and hath been lately concluded and settled by both Parliaments; we shall each one of us, according to our place and interest, endeavour that they may remain conjoined in a firm peace and union to all posterity; and that justice may be done upon the wilful opposers thereof, in manner expressed in the precedent article.

VI. We shall also, according to our places and callings, in this common cause of religion, liberty, and peace of the kingdoms, assist and defend all those that enter into this League and Covenant, in the maintaining and pursuing thereof; and shall not suffer ourselves, directly or indirectly, by whatsoever combination, persuasion, or terror, to be divided and withdrawn from this blessed union and conjunction, whether to make defection to the contrary part, or to give ourselves to a detestable indifference or neutrality in this cause which so much concerneth the glory of GOD, the good of the kingdom, and honour of the King; but shall, all the days of our lives, zealously and constantly continue therein against all opposition, and promote the same, according to our power, against all lets and impediments whatsoever, and, what we are not able ourselves to suppress or overcome, we shall reveal and make known, that it may be timely prevented or removed: All which we shall do as in the sight of God.

And, because these kingdoms are guilty of many sins and provocations against GOD, and his Son JESUS CHRIST, as is too manifest by our present distresses and dangers, the fruits thereof; we profess and declare before GOD and the world, our unfeigned desire to be humbled for our own sins, and for the sins of these kingdoms: especially, that we have not as we ought valued the inestimable benefit of the gospel; that we have not laboured for the purity and power thereof; and that we have not endeavoured to receive CHRIST in our hearts, nor to walk worthy of him in our lives; which are the causes of other sins and transgressions so much abounding amongst us: and our true and unfeigned purpose, desire, and endeavour for ourselves, and all others under our power and charge, both in publick and in private, in all duties we owe to GOD and man, to amend our lives, and each one to go before another in the example of a real reformation; that the Lord may turn away his wrath and heavy indignation, and establish these churches and kingdoms in truth and peace. And this Covenant we make in the presence of ALMIGHTY GOD, the Searcher of all hearts, with a true intention to perform the same, as we shall answer at that great day when the secrets of all hearts shall be disclosed; most humbly beseeching the Lord to strengthen us by his HOLY SPIRIT for this end, and to bless our desires and proceedings with such success, as may be deliverance and safety to his people, and encouragement to other Christian churches, groaning under, or in danger of, the yoke of antichristian tyranny, to join in the same or like association and covenant, to the glory of GOD, the enlargement of the kingdom of JESUS CHRIST, and the peace and tranquility of Christian kingdoms and commonwealths.

Victorious Conquerors!

God makes all his children conquerors. They conquer themselves; *fortior est qui se quam qui fortissima vincit moenia* [he who conquers himself is stronger than he who conquerors the stoutest ramparts]. The saints conquer their own lusts; they bind these princes in fetters of iron. Psa cxlix 8. Though the children of God may be sometimes foiled, and lose a single battle, yet not the victory. They conquer the world. The world holds forth her two breasts of profit and pleasure, and many are overcome by it; but the children of God have a world-conquering faith. 'This is the victory that overcometh the world, even our faith.' I John v 4. They conquer their enemies. How can that be, when their enemies often take away their lives? They conquer, by not complying with them; as the three children would not fall down to the golden image. Dan iii 18. They would rather burn than bow. Thus they were conquerors. He who complies to another's lust, is a captive; he who refuses to comply, is a conqueror. God's children conquer their enemies by heroic patience. A patient Christian, like the anvil, bears all strokes invincibly. Thus the martyrs overcame their enemies by patience. God's children are more than conquerors. 'are more than conquerors.' Rom viii 37. How are they more than conquerors? Because they conquer without loss, and because they are crowned after death, which other conquerors are not.

–Thomas Watson[1]

---

[1] Thomas Watson, The Lord's Prayer, The Banner of Truth Trust, London, 1972, page 22.

Alexander Henderson
The John Knox of The 2nd Reformation

The Solemn League and Covenant of 1643 were sworn to in St. Margaret's Church at Westminster. Assembled were 220 members of the House of Commons and of the Westminster divines. This covenant consisted of an oath, "to be subscribed by all persons in both kingdoms, whereby they bound themselves to preserve the Reformed religion in the Church of Scotland, in doctrine, worship, discipline, and government, according to the Word of God and practice of the best Reformed Churches . . ." It was hoped that this would unite the churches of all three of the kingdoms.

The Covenanters were crusaders for Christ. They desired that Christ would be on the throne of the country that they loved. They fought for the rights of King Jesus, for whom "No peril was too hazardous, no sacrifice too great." Alexander Henderson was a foremost and most statesmanlike of the Presbyterian ministers of that day. He took a great part in writing the National Covenant which was a reproduction of an earlier covenant of 1581. It condemned prelacies and confirmed the faith of the Reformed Church. Henderson wrote the section of protest against the alien modes of worship.

There was also the National Covenant of 1638 was called the Magna Charta of the Presbyterian Church, or of Scottish Liberty. It said in part: "...from the knowledge and conscience of our duty to God, to our King and country, . . . we promise and swear, by the great name of the Lord our God, to continue in the profession and obedience of the foresaid religion, and that we shall defend the same, and resist all these contrary errors and corruptions, according to our vocation, and to the uttermost of the power that God hath put in our hands, all the days of our life." Thousands gathered in the church yard of the Greyfriars, February 28, 1938. Nobles and barons, ministers and common people heard an address by the Earl of Loudoun, and prayer by Alexander Henderson. Later, fifty-three Presbyteries were represented at an Assembly meeting, Henderson being the Moderator. They annulled the previous Assembly concerning Episcopacy, swept away the Service Book and Articles, and excommunicated eight Bishops. The National Covenant was confirmed and Presbyterianism rose from the ashes strong and true.

The spiritual life of Alexander did not start out upon that strong rock of God's Word. He first embraced the Prelacy. Alexander Henderson received his degrees from the university with honors. The Archbishop of St. Andrews appointed him to be a minister of Leuchars, in the Shire of Fife. However, the people of that parish did not want him, and so, on the day of his ordination, they shut fast the doors of the church. The Bishop and Henderson had to break in by a window. Soon after there was a report that a communion service was to be held in the neighborhood, and Robert Bruce was to preach. Alexander went secretly to the church, finding a dark corner in which to sit and watch. Bruce came to the pulpit, and after a long moment of silence, Alexander heard these words, "He

that entereth not by the door, but climbeth up some other way, the same is a thief and a robber."

By the blessing of God and the effectual working of the Holy Spirit, Alexander Henderson's heart was moved, and the first step of conversion to Christ was taken. He became a faithful and diligent minister of the Gospel, a loyal Presbyterian, and a steady hand in carrying out the covenantal work of the Reformation, from 1638 to his death.

In 1637 a new Anglo-Popish liturgy and Service book was prepared and imposed upon the Protestant Church. On July 23, 1637, it was introduced to the Greyfriar's Church, Edinburgh. As Bishop Argyle officiated, the people let their feelings be known through tears and groans. In St. Giles another incident occurred. The Dean of Edinburgh, arrayed in splendid robes, began to read the prayers. An old woman, Janet Geddes, snatched up the stool upon which she was sitting, and hurled it at his head, exclaiming, "Villain, dost thou say mass at my lug (ear)?" Such sparks made the Archbishop of St. Andrews exclaim, "All that we have been doing these 30 years past is at once thrown down."

Refusing to buy and use the Service Book, and the Book of Canons imposed upon the church by King Charles I, Alexander was brought up on charges by the Archbishop of St. Andrews. After he and others sent petitions and complaints to the Council, showing the sinfulness of such impositions, he was charged to leave Edinburgh within twenty-four hours. After his death one of his close friends, Mr. Baille, spoke to the General Assembly of 1647, saying, "May I be permitted to conclude with my earnest wish, that that glorious soul of worthy memory, who is now crowned with the reward of all his labours for God and us, may be fragrant among us, as long as till the coming of our Lord. You know he spent his strength, wore out his days, and did breathe out his life in the service of God, and of this Church. This binds it on us and posterity to account him the fairest ornament, after John Knox of incomparable memory, that ever the Church of Scotland did enjoy."

Alexander Peden
His prayers were conversations!

Alexander Peden was a native of Ayrshire, born about 1626 in the parish of Sorn. After attending the University he worked as a schoolmaster, precentor, and Session clerk under the minister of the Gospel at Tarbolton, John Guthrie. He later became a minister at Glenluce in Galloway. After three years he went to the pulpit for the last time, preaching from Acts 20. It was night when he concluded his message. As he left the pulpit, closing the pulpit door behind him, he took his Bible and banged the top of the door three times, saying, "I arrest thee in my Master's name, that none ever enter here but such as come in by the door as I have done."

While at Galloway, Peden was seen as a man of fervent prayer and powerful in the preaching of the Gospel for the salvation of souls. It is said that "his prayers were conversations with a personal friend." His sermons were "visions of the glory of God which had come to him in his meditations, and filled the people with awe."

In 1666 an edict was issued against Alexander Peden by the Council. He was charged with holding conventicles, preaching, and baptizing children in Kilmarnock and Croigie parishes and Castlehill. Mr. Peden was considered a prophet of the Lord, for many of his predictions came true. He should certainly be counted among those, whose prayer life was intense, and whose life was guided by the Spirit of God in a most marvelous and personal way.

There was the time when Peden and Welch and the Laird of Glenover were traveling the road, and a small group of soldiers, dragoons, came from the direction they were traveling. Peden said to his friends, "Keep up your good courage and confidence, for God hast laid an arrest on these men, that they should do us no harm." They were looking for Peden. He rode toward the soldiers and was asked if he knew about a certain road. He directed them in the right way and returned to his friends. Asked why he had not sent the lad instead of placing himself in danger, Peden replied, "For I knew they would be like Egyptian dogs, they could not move a tongue against me, my time being not yet come." Mr. Peden preached in both Ireland and Scotland. Because he was being hunted down by the Council he went to the fields, living in the caves for fear that a household would also be persecuted if he accepted their hospitality.

While preaching on a hillside, Peden and the Congregation saw the dragoons coming toward them. They had spread out hoping to imprison all of them. After prayer, Peden encouraged the congregation to remain calm, saying, "Friends, the bitterest of this blast is over; we will be no more troubled with them this day." In their fear he called them to prayer. The answer came in the form of clouds of mist which rose from the hillsides and enveloped the dragoons and the Covenanters. The Covenanters knew the area and easily escaped the soldiers while they remained frozen on their horses, not knowing which way to turn. In the hearts of the Covenanters Alexander Peden became known as "Peden, the Prophet."

In June of 1673 Peden stayed with Hugh Ferguson of Knockdew in Carrick. Mr. Ferguson had insisted that he stay the night. Peden declared that this would be "a dear night's quarters" for both of them. The dragoons heard that Peden was at this home, and both he and Hugh were carried to prison at Edinburgh. Hugh Ferguson was fined 1000 merks. Alexander Peden was later sent to Bass and imprisoned. In prison Peden continued to witness to the Gospel of His Lord Jesus Christ. He was mocked while at prison. One day a guard passed his cell, saying, "The devil take him." Peden responded, "Thou knowest not what thou art saying; but thou shalt repent that." He continued to speak to the guard and then pray for him. By the next morning the guard was in deep conviction of his guilt before God. He repented of his sins. He was again commanded to bear his arms against the Covenanters. He refused to lift arms against Christ, "I have done that too long." He became a most singular Christian with his family, settling in East Lothian.

Peden was once banished to the American colonies. While on the ship, he told his fellow travelers that they would soon find freedom in London. When the ship docked at London, the captains of both ships refused to take them. They were freed in London. Peden was past sixty years of age when the Lord took him home. Just before his death he had left his cave and went to his brother's home. The cave was discovered by the enemy, but they would no longer trouble him in this world. He had prophesied once more: "They will not find me alive though they search twenty times this house." He died the next day. He was known for his piety, zeal, and faithfulness to the preaching of the Gospel. As to his prophecies, one wrote, "Abundance of this good man's predictions are well-known to be already come to pass."

Alexander Peden was buried in the private vaults in the laird of Auchinleck's isle. However, a troop of solders came and lifted his corpse, hanging it on gallows of Cumnock. The Countess of Dumfires interceded with the Council, and had his body buried at the foot of the gibbet. Others, to the honor of Peden, were asked to be buried beside him. A thorn bush was planted at his head and another at his feet. From a sermon of 1682 we hear this testimony of Alexander Peden: "For you, poor, broken-hearted followers of Christ, to whom He hath given grace to follow Him in the storm, I tell you, Grace is your glory. At your first conversion our Lord gives you the one end of the line but he keeps the other end in glory with Himself. But, sirs, He will have you all there at length."

Trust and Rest in the Lord
Psalm 37:3-16[1]

Set thou thy trust upon the Lord, and be thou doing good;
And so thou in the land shalt dwell, and verily have food.
Delight thyself in God; he'll give thine heart's desire to thee.
Thy way to God commit, him trust, it bring to pass shall be.
And, like unto the light, he shall thy righteousness display;
And he thy judgment shall bring forth like noon-tide of the day.
Rest in the Lord, and patiently wait for him: do not fret
For him who, prosp'ring in his way, success in sin doth get.
Do thou from anger cease, and wrath see thou forsake also:
Fret not thyself in any wise, that evil thou should'st do.
For those that evil doers are shall be cut off and fall:
But those that wait upon the Lord the earth inherit shall.
For yet a little while, and then the wicked shall not be;
His place thou shalt consider well, but if thou shalt not see.
But by inheritance the earth the meek ones shall possess:
They also shall delight themselves in an abundant peace.
The wicked plots against the just, and at him whets his teeth:
The Lord shall laugh at him, because his day he cometh seeth.
The wicked have drawn out the sword, and bent their bow, to slay
The poor and needy, and to kill men of an upright way.
But their own sword, which they have drawn, shall enter their own heart:
Their bows which they have bent shall break, and into pieces part.
A little that a just man hath is more and better far
Than is the wealth of many such as lewd and wicked are.

---

[1] Psalm 37, The Comprehensive Psalter, Scottish Metrical Version, Blue Banner Books, A Ministry of First Presbyterian Church, Rowlett, Texas, 2000, pages 73-74.

We serve Christ

The friends of truth, the subjects of Him who is King in Zion, must stand prepared to surrender the applause of man whose breath is in his nostrils; must value, above everything, the approbation of the Almighty; and aim, at all times, at being able to say in sincerity, *We serve the Lord Christ.* By taking a decided stand on their own proper ground, without being moved from it by the dread of singularity, and without suffering themselves to be swallowed up in the devouring vortex of party life, or of latitudinarian indifference, their very position of apparent neutrality will carry in it a distinct and palpable testimony for the truth as it is Jesus. *Prove all things, hold fast that which is good. Wherefore take unto you the whole armour of God, that ye may be able to withstand in the evil day, and having done all to stand. Stand, therefore, having your loins girt about with truth, and having on the breastplate of righteousness, and your feet shod with the preparation of the Gospel of peace. Behold, I come quickly: hold fast which thou hast, that no man take thy crown!*
–William Symington[1]

[1] <u>Messiah the Prince</u>, ibid, page 209.

John Welch
A man who imitated Christ

John Welch was born in 1570. His father, Laird of Collieston, owned a large estate in Nithsdale. John's life would become a rich example of grace and mercy. However, as a child, he was a regular truant from school. He was but a youth when he left his father's house to join a band of thieves. He made his living with those who survived by robbing from both sides of the border. John soon found himself in rags as he practiced the prodigal's misery. He then resolved to return to his father's house and plead for reconciliation. He traveled to Dumfries where he found shelter under the roof of his aunt, Mrs. Agnes Forsyth. He begged her to be a mediator between himself and his father. Providence brought his father to visit Agnes. She asked him if he had any news of his son. To which the father replied, "O Cruel woman, how can you name him to me! The first news I expect to hear of him is, that he is hanged as a thief."

The father then asked Agnes if she had heard if his son was alive. She said yes, comforting him with the thought that perhaps his son would be a better man than a boy. Agnes then called John, who came weeping and beseeching his father for forgiveness. His father began to reproach him. Yet at length, with tears and the help of Mrs. Forsyth, he was persuaded to be reconciled to his son. John entreated his father to send him to college, and there to test his behavior. John went home with his father, was sent to college, and there revealed himself to be a good student and a sincere convert to Christ.

His first ministry was at Selkirk. He preached the Word faithfully and proved to be a worthy opponent of wickedness. He also showed himself to be a man of prayer. From this time until his death he felt the day ill-spent if he stayed not seven or eight hours in prayer. Ewart, an old man of Selkirk, remembered Mr. Welch as a "type of Christ," meaning that he imitated Christ in the many things he did. John preached publicly once a day, spending the rest of the day in other spiritual exercises. His ministry was received with great tenderness.

In the year 1590 John Welch went to Ayr, staying until he was banished by King James. Ayr was not a place where any man could feel safe. Ayr was so filled with factions and bloody conflicts that no one could walk its streets with safety. Yet in this city, John became an example of a gracious mediator. Wearing heavy head gear John would step between two parties of warring men. Little by little he made Ayr a peaceful habitation. Mr. Welch would, after ending a skirmish among his neighbors, reconcile them by bringing the enemies to a table which he prepared in the street. Beginning with prayer, he would persuade them to profess themselves to be friends. He ended his work with the singing of a psalm. John became the people's counselor, and an example to imitate.

John's grace was also seen in his dealing with an aged minister of Ayr, Mr. Porterfield. The easy disposition of Mr. Porterfield led him into many dangerous practices. One was that he regularly attended the bow butts and Archery on Sabbath afternoons. John Welch reclaimed him with gentleness. He, along with his two closes friends, John Stuart and Hugh Kennedy, spent Sabbath afternoons in conference and prayer. They invited Mr. Porterfield to these Sabbath exercises, which he could not refuse. By this means Porterfield was diverted from his former sinful practices, and brought to a more Christ-like behavior.

John Welch married Elizabeth Knox, daughter of the great Scots Reformer, John Knox. John Welch remained a man of prayer, Elizabeth witnessing his rising in the night to kneel before God. He would continually wrestle with God, asking Him to grant him Scotland.

King James VI came to the throne and purposed to destroy the Church of Scotland. He appointed bishops to corrupt the Church. He desired to hasten his goal by destroying the General Assemblies. In 1605 he issued a letter disbanding the Assembly. However, many faithful ministers gathered together as an Assembly knowing that without such a hedge against the government, the corruption of doctrine would soon follow. Though Mr. Welch did not attend the Assembly, because of his support of the ministers, he was gathered up with others to face the trial of treason.

Mr. Welch soon ended up in Blackness Castle, where prisoners of well-to-do families were put. This fortress still stands today. The Blackness is situated just west of Edinburgh on the southern shore. John Welch was tried for high treason and was banished from Scotland. He would travel to France, and there, minister faithfully for Christ for sixteen years. While John Welch was in Blackness, he wrote to a Lilias Graham, Countess of Wigton. Here are a few of his words of testimony: "Now, let it be so that I have fought my fight, and run my race, and now from henceforth is laid up for me that crown of righteousness, which the Lord, that righteous God, will give; and not to me only, but to all that love His appearance, and choose to witness this, that Jesus Christ is the King of saints, and that His church is a most free kingdom, yea, as free as any kingdom under heaven . . . " John Welch affirmed the crown of Christ, his scepter, and kingdom. His desire was to have the Lord's hand, to do with him whatsoever would "please His Majesty."

At the time of his last sickness he was heard to say, "O Lord, hold Thy hand, it is enough; thy servant is a clay vessel, and can hold no more." John spent his last days in London, going to meet his Lord in 1681.

Song from God's Word

Advancing Still
[Psalm 84, melita.88.88.88.][1]

Advancing still from strength to strength
They go where other pilgrims trod,
Till each to Zion comes at length
And stands before the face of God.
LORD God of hosts, my pleading hear;
O Jacob's God, to me give ear.

Look Thou, O God, upon our shield;
The face of Thine Anointed see;
One day within Thy courts will yield
More good than thousands without Thee.
I'd rather stand near my God's house
Than dwell in tents of wickedness.

For God the LORD is shield and sun;
The LORD will grace and glory give.
No good will He withhold from one
Who does uprightly walk and live.
O LORD of hosts, how blest is he
Who places all his trust in Thee!

---

[1] The Book of Psalms for Singing, Crown and Covenant Pub., Psalm 84B.

Walk in Christ

As ye have therefore received Christ Jesus the Lord, so walk ye in him: Rooted and built up in him, and established in the faith, as ye have been taught, abounding therein with thanksgiving.

–Colossians 1:6-7

Look unto Jesus

Wherefore seeing we also are compassed about with so great a cloud of witnesses, let us lay aside every weight, and the sin which doth so easily beset us, and let us run with patience the race that is set before us, looking unto Jesus the author and finisher of our faith; who for the joy that was set before him endured the cross, despising the shame, and is set down at the right hand of the throne of God.

–Hebrews 12:1-2

Christ our Savior

5. The Lord Jesus, by His perfect obedience, and sacrifice of Himself, which He, through the eternal Spirit, once offered up unto God, hath fully satisfied the justice of His Father; and purchased, not only reconciliation, but an everlasting inheritance in the kingdom of heaven, for all those whom the Father hath given unto Him.

8. To all those for whom Christ hath purchased redemption, He doth certainly and effectually apply and communicate the same, making intercession for them, and revealing unto them, in and by the Word, the mysteries of salvation, effectually persuading them by His Spirit to believe and obey, and governing their hearts by His Word and Spirit, overcoming all their enemies by is almighty power and wisdom, in such manner, and ways, as are most consonant to His wonderful and unsearchable dispensation.[1]

---

[1] Westminster Confession of Faith, ibid, Of Christ the Mediator, pages 50-51.

John Bunyan
A Tinker's Pilgrimage

John Bunyan is remembered for his "Pilgrims Progress." Mr. Bunyan was born in the year 1628 at Harrowden, near Bedford (parish of Elstow), England. He should also be remembered and counted among those who were 'faithful unto death,' as he too was imprisoned for the preaching of the gospel. It is recorded that he was influenced by Martin's Luther's *Commentary on the Epistle to the Galatians*."

Martin Luther also knew what it meant to be hounded by the enemies of God. His Hymn spoke to those who lived the 'Martyr's Life,' the time of the Reformation when the faith of our Lord's saints was being tested:

"A safe stronghold our God is still—[1]
A trusty shield and weapon:
He'll help us clear from all the ill
That hath us now o'ertaken.
The ancient prince of hell
Hath risen with purpose fell;
Strong mail of craft and power
He weareth in this hour—
"With force of arms we nothing can;
Full soon were we down-ridden;
But for us fights the proper man.
Whom God himself hath bidden.
Ask ye, Who is this same?
Jesus Christ is his name,
The Lord Zebaoth's son
He, and no other one,
Shall conquer in the battle.
"And were this world all devils o'er,
And watching to devour us,
We lay it not to heart so sore—
We know they can't o'erpower us.
And let the prince of ill
Look grim as o'er he will,
He harms us not a whit,

---

[1] "At a time when the cause of the Reformation appeared to be in jeopardy, Luther composed a hymn in German, full of sentiments of the most lively faith. This is still a favourite in many parts of Germany, and is sung with great effect, on the occasions of public celebrations. We give it in Carlyle's translation, which though somewhat quaint, is true to the expression and spirit of the original,--Editor, <u>The Covenanter</u>, Belfast, Vol. II, page 331.

> For why? His doom is writ.
> "God's Word for all their craft and force,
> One moment will not linger,
> But, in spite of hell, shall have its course—
> 'Tis written by His finger,—
> And though they take our life,
> Goods, houses, children, wife,
> Yet is their profit small;
> These things shall vanish all—
> God's city it remaineth."

John Bunyan's life was a journey of faith by which he learned the majestic truth of the grace of God. Bunyan's 'Pilgrim's Progress' reveal his advancing from strength to strength in the grace of God. To remind us that the controversy of whether works must be added to faith for justification is not new, we find Christian having a discussion with  Ignorance. Christian asks Ignorance, "How dost thou believe?" Ignorance answers, "I believe that Christ died for sinners; and that I shall be justified before God from the curse through his gracious acceptance of my obedience to his law. O Thus: Christ makes my duties, that are religious, acceptable to his Father by virtue of his mercies; and so shall I be justified." Christian answers, "1. Thou believest with a fantastical faith; for this faith is nowhere described in the word. 2. Thou believest with a false faith; because it takes justification from the personal righteousness of Christ, and applies it thy own. 3. This faith maketh not Christ a justifier of thy person, but of thy actions sake, which is false. 4. Therefore this faith is deceitful, even such as will leave thee under wrath in the day of God Almighty; for true justifying faith puts the soul, as sensible of its lost condition by the law, upon flying for refuge unto Christ's righteousness (which righteousness of his is not an act of grace by which he maketh, for justification, thy obedience accepted with God, but his personal obedience to the law, in doing and suffering for us what that required at our hands); this righteousness, I say, true faith accepteth; under the skirt of which the soul being shrouded, and by it presented as spotless before God, it is accepted, and acquitted from condemnation."

John Bunyan knew the majesty of the grace of God because he knew himself to be a great sinner. It is recorded that he said of himself, "I was a town sinner; I was the vilest in the country, a Jerusalem sinner; murdering the Son of God afresh by my ungodly deeds, and putting him to open shame."[1] Bunyan was baptized about the year 1655 and admitted as a member of the church at Bedford. Through trials and temptations the Lord was sharpening a dull soul to be a living soul for service. Thus it is said of him, "And God was pleased to bless and prosper the work of his hand, so that many souls were brought to lay hold upon the Lord Jesus, by believing, and to the receiving of truth in the love thereof, through his ministry, to the praise and glory of God's grace."[2]

John Bunyan, having preached the gospel for five years, was seized and placed before a justice of the peace, who committed him to prison. He could have been released until the trial, but he refused to obey the judge that he would not preach to the people. Bunyan was indicted as "an upholder and maintainer of unlawful assemblies and conventicles, and for not conforming to the Church of England."

The biographer continues with "a taste of" of Bunyan's experience in prison, during which time he wrote several treatises, *The Holy City; Christian Behaviour, The Resurrection of the Dead; and Grace Abounding to the Chief of Sinners.* Bunyan "professed he never had so great an inlet, in all his life, into the word of God as then." Of Christ he said, "For there I have seen him and felt him indeed." It was in prison "that God gave him sweet and precious sights—the forgiveness of his sins, and of his being with Jesus in another world; yea, here it was that he found, upon every temptation, that God stood by him and rebuked the tempter."

After twelve years of suffering in prison, a Dr. Barlow, Bishop of Lincoln used his influence to free Bunyan. He continued preaching the gospel, helping those in need and comforting the sick. "He looked upon this life as a delay of that blessedness which his soul was aspiring to, and thirsting after; and in this holy longing frame of spirit, after a sickness of ten days, he breathed out his soul into the hands of his blessed Redeemer, following his happy Pilgrim from the City of Destruction to he heavenly Jerusalem."

John Bunyan writes of his imprisonment that is was on November 12, 1660 when he was invited to teach in Bedfordshire; the justice Francis

---

[1] Pilgrim's Progress, Life of John Bunyan, pages iii-xxv, William Collins, Sons, London and Glasgow.

[2] Pilgrim's Progress, Life of John Bunyan, ibid. This story is also recorded of Bunyan the tinker, "that being to preach in a church in a country village (before the restoration of King Charles) in Cambridgeshire, and the people being gathered together in the churchyard, a Cambridge scholar, and none the soberest of them neither, inquired what the meaning of that concourse of people was, (it being a week day;) and being told that one Bunyan, a tinker was to preach there, he gave a boy twopence to hold his horse, saying, 'He was resolved to hear the tinker prate;' and so he went into the church resolved to hear him. But God met him in the ministry, so that he came out much changed, and would by this good will hear none but the tinker for a long time after, he himself becoming a very eminent preacher in that country afterwards."

Wingate issued a warrant for his arrest.[1] When the constable came into where a small group of Christians were meeting, he "found us only with our Bibles in our hands, ready to speak and hear the word of God, for we were just about to begin our exercise. Nay, we had begun our opportunity, intending to have preached the word of the Lord unto them there present, but the constable' coming in prevented us. So that I was taken and forced to depart the room." This was not a surprise, for when coming to his friend's house he was told of some whispering that a warrant was out for his arrest. Asked if they should call off the meeting, Bunyan replied, "No, by no means; I will not stir, neither will I have the meeting dismissed for this: Come, be of good cheer, let us not be daunted; our cause is good, we need not be ashamed of it; to preach God's word, it is so good a work that we shall be well rewarded if we suffer for that; of to his purpose." Waiting in prison for his trial, Bunyan wrote, "Let the rage and malice of men be never so great, they can do no more not go no further than God permits them; but when they have done their worst, we know all things shall work together for good to them that love God. Farewell!"

Faithful Magistrate

Diabolus, after he had ended his flattering and deceitful speech, by which he hoped to win over the town, added this threat, "How, then, shall Mansoul think to escape my hand and force?" The lord mayor of Mansoul, of the country of Universe, answered him: "O Diabolus, prince of darkness and master of all deceit! Thy lying flatteries we have had and made sufficient probation of, and have tasted too deeply of that destructive cup already; should we, therefore, again hearken unto thee, and so break the commandment of our great Shaddai to join affinity with thee, would not our Prince reject us and cast us off for ever? And being cast off by him, can the place that he has prepared for thee be a place of rest for us? Besides, O thou that art empty and void of all truth! We are rather ready to die by thy hand than to fall in with thy flattering and lying deceits."[2]

---

[1] The Complete Works of John Bunyan, Bradley, Garretson & Co., Philadelphia, 1874, "A Relation of the imprisonment of Mr. John Bunyan" (written by himself), pages 677-690. [Picture of prison and bridge copied from same book.]
[2] Ibid, The Holy War, page 453.

The Pilgrim's Progress

When Christian and Faithful[1] found themselves in Vanity Fair,[2] they soon found themselves before the court. Called heretic and traitor, Faithful testified to the truth of the Word of God, saying, among other things, "that in the worship of God there is required a divine faith; but there can be no divine faith without a divine revelation of the will of God."

The false witnesses were brought forward at their trial, and the jury was stacked with men like Mr. Blindman, Mr. No-good, Mr. Hate-light and Mr. Liar. The judge instructed the jury as to their responsibility to hang him or save his life. However, it was according to their law. For they were reminded of the deeds of Daniel and his friends and how they broke the king's law in word and deed, "which must, therefore, needs be intolerable." The twisting of the Word of God by the enemy of Christ is not foreign to us today. "He is a rogue," said Mr. Liar. "Hanging is too good for him," said Mr. Cruelty. Mr. Implacable said, "Might I have all the world given me, I could not be reconciled to him; therefore let us forthwith bring him in guilty of death."[3] So according to their law they scourged Faithful, stoned him, and "burned him to ashes at the stake." It was then that John Bunyan saw in his dream "that there stood behind the multitude a chariot and a couple of horses waiting for Faithful, who ... was taken up into it, and straightway was carried up through the clouds, with sound of trumpet, the nearest way to the Celestial Gate." Christian spent some time in jail, "But He who overrules all things, having the power of their rage in his own hand, so wrought it about, that Christian went his way."

Christian sang as he went, saying—

> Well, Faithful, thou hast faithfully profest
> Unto thy Lord, with whom thou shalt be blest;
> When faithless ones, with all their vain delights,
> Are crying out under their hellish plights.

---

[1] John Bunyan, The Pilgrim's Progress, William Collins, Sons, & CO, Ltd, London and Glasgow.

[2] There was a 'vanity fair' at Ephesus [Acts 19:23-41] where Demetrius, a silversmith and maker of shrines for Diana, call the traders together, saying, "Men, you know that we have our prosperity by this trade." They came face to face with the Gospel of the Christ and His way of righteousness!

[3] "A blessed verdict! Well worthy of every pilgrim to obtain. Reader, do you profess to be one? See, then, that you study to act so to gain such a verdict from such a jury; and then be sure Christ will soon pronounce upon thee is Euge, O Brave! 'Well done, thou good and faithful servant! Enter thou into the joy of thy Lord' (Matt. Xxv. 21)." –notes by Rev. Mason, The Pilgrims Progress, ibid.

Sing, Faithful, sing, and let thy name survive!
For though they kill'd thee, thou are yet alive.

John Calvin wrote of *Bearing the cross in persecution,*[1] "Now, to suffer persecution for righteousness sake is a singular comfort. For it ought to occur to us how much honor God bestows upon us in thus furnishing us with the special badge of his soldiery. I say that not only they who labor for the defense of the gospel but they who in any way maintain the cause of righteousness suffer persecution for righteousness. Therefore, whether in declaring God's truth against Satan's falsehoods or in taking up the protection of the good and the innocent against the wrongs of the wicked, we must undergo the offences and hatred of the world, which may imperil either our life, or fortunes, or our honor. Let us not grieve or be troubled in thus far devoting our efforts to God, or count ourselves miserable in those matters in which he has with his own lips declared us blessed [Matt. 5:10[2]]."

Calvin encourages us, that *Suffering under the cross, the Christian finds consolation in God;* "Scripture, then by these and like warnings give us abundant comfort in either the disgrace or the calamity we bear for the sake of defending righteousness. Consequently, we are too ungrateful if we do not willingly and cheerfully undergo these things at the Lord's hand; especially since this sort of cross most properly belongs to believers, and by it Christ wills to be glorified in us, as Peter teaches [I Peter 4:12 ff.]."[3]

> *"Beloved, think it not strange concerning the fiery trial which is to try you, as though some strange thing happened unto you; but rejoice, inasmuch as ye are partakers of Christ's sufferings; that, when his glory shall be revealed, ye may be glad also with exceeding joy. If ye be reproached for the name of Christ, happy are ye; for the spirit of glory and of God resteth upon you; on their part he is evil spoken of, but on your part he is glorified."*
>
> 1 Peter 4:12-14

---

[1] Calvin, Institutes of the Christian Religion, ibid, Book III, page 707

[2] "Blessed are they which are persecuted for righteousness sake; for theirs is the kingdom of heaven. Blessed are ye, when men shall revile you, and persecute you, and shall say all manner of evil against you falsely, for my sake. Rejoice and be exceeding glad; for great is your reward in heaven; for so persecuted they the prophets which were before you" [Matt. 5:10-12].

[3] Calvin, Institutes of the Christian Religion, ibid, page 708.

William Tyndale
Schoolmaster and Martyr of Christ

William Tyndale was born about the year 1500 on the borders of Wales. At an early age Tyndale was sent to the University of Oxford where he applied himself to the study of Scriptures and in the knowledge of languages. He became acquainted with the writings of Luther and Erasmus, privately instructing other students in the truths of Scripture. Because of his abilities he received an appointment in Cardinal Wolsey's newly-founded college. However, being suspected of Lutheranism, he was compelled to leave the University. He went to Cambridge, where he became schoolmaster to the children of Master John Welch, a knight of Gloucestershire, whose dinner table was shared with doctors and clergy and other learned men, who were strenuous supporters of the papacy. Master Tyndale took much advantage of sitting at the same table with these men, as they discussed questions on the Scriptures and controversies written by Luther and Erasmus; Tyndale "spared not to show unto them simply and plainly his judgment, and when they at any time did vary from Tyndale in opinions, he would show them in the Book, and lay plainly before them the open and manifest places of the Scriptures, to confute their errors and confirm his sayings. And thus continued they for a certain season, reasoning and contending together divers times, until at length they waxed weary, and bare a secret grudge in their hearts against him."[1]

The knight and lady Welch were surprised at the boldness of Tyndale. One day they returned from a banquet to which they were invited by some important ecclesiastics. They shared the arguments advanced by these priests. Tyndale answered the arguments maintaining the truth of Scriptures and reproving their false opinions. Lady Welch responded by pointing out the high position of those at the banquet and therefore, to Tyndale, "were it reason, think you, that we should believe you before them?"  Tyndale chose to answer her argument by giving to them his translation of a discourse written by Erasmus, titled "The Manual of a Christian Soldier." John and Lady Welch were so impressed by the writing that they no longer entertained or gave "countenance to the ignorant and immoral Romish doctors."

---

[1] <u>Foxes Book of Martyrs</u>, W.B. Forbush, ed, Zondervan Publishing house, Grand Rapids, MI, 1970, page 176.

Tyndale was soon summoned to appear before the Chancellor of the Diocese. He "prayed earnestly to God to give him strength to stand fast in the truth of his word. He was protected; none of his accusers came forward, and he was dismissed with a reprimand." There were those who questioned the rule of the pope, defying his works; and those who were tormented by Tyndale's arguments; one breaking out with these blasphemous words. "We had better be without God's laws than the pope's." Tyndale's answer speaks of the Word of God that was being unchained, and how God used him in opening the truth given by God alone: "'I defy the pope, and all his laws;' adding, that if God spared his life, ere many years he would cause the boys that drove the plough to know more of the scripture than his opponent."

Tyndale left Cambridge and traveled to London, the threat against having gained momentum. He was determined to translate the Scriptures into the English language. Part of his introduction to the translation of the first five Books of the Bible, speaks of his desire that the people should read the Bible in their tongue: "Because I had perceived by experience that it was impossible to establish the lay people in any truth, except the scriptures were plainly laid before their eyes in their mother tongue, that they might see the process, order, and meaning of the text: for else, whatsoever truth is taught them, these enemies of all truth quench it again, partly with the smoke of their bottomless pit, whereof thou readest in the Apocalypse, chap. Ix.; that is, with apparent reasons of sophistry, and traditions of their own making, founded without ground of scripture, and partly in juggling with the text, expounding it in such a sense as in impossible to gather from the text, if thou see the process, order, and meaning thereof."[1]

Master Tyndale remained in London for almost a year, living with a Humphrey Monmouth, who gave him lodging and food. Night and Day he studied and ate little. Humphrey was later imprisoned for assisting Tyndale. When he was released Humphrey continued to support those who preached the truth. He died in 1537 after serving as alderman and sheriff.

Tyndale traveled to Saxony where he met Luther and others of the Reformation. He settled at Antwerp where he found support from several English merchants who were favorable to the truth. He continued his translation of the Bible with the help of Frith and Roye. An edition of fifteen copies of the New Testament were printed in 1526 and sent to England. The Romish prelates vented their anger at Tyndale; Tonstal, Bishop of London, commanding that the translations of the Bible and

---

[1] The Lives of the British Reformers, Presbyterian Board of Publication, Philadelphia, Pa., page 3 of *Some Account of the Life of William Tindal* (Tyndale) chapter.

other writings of Tyndale should be gathered together along with the writings of Luther. Fox observed that "These books of W. Tyndale, being compiled, published, and sent over into England, it cannot be spoken what a door of light they opened to the eyes of the whole English nation, which before were many years shut up in darkness."

The Lord blessed the translation of His Word by providing financial assistance from the enemy. Bishop Cuthbert Tonstal and Sir Thomas More sought to work out a method by which to destroy what they labeled 'that false erroneous translation' of Tyndale. Bishop Tonstal consulted with a merchant by the name of Augustine Packington, who traded between London and Antwerp, on how Tyndale's translations could be delivered into his hands. Packington was a secret friend of Tyndale and knew his need of money. It is said that the Bishop wished to stop the dispersion of the Bible without resorting to the cruel measures of others. Packington thought that a good means of helping Tyndale, he suggested to the Bishop that he would endeavor to purchase all the books, assuring him that he would have every book that is printed and unsold. The Bishop, "thinking that he had God 'by the toe,' said, 'Dour diligence, gentle Master Packington! get them for me, and I will pay whatsoever they cost; for I intend to burn and destroy them all at Paul's Cross.'"[1] Declaring the matter to Tyndale, Packington took the books to the Bishop. And so, Tyndale had the money to continue his translation and printing to the vexation of the Bishop, who once again paid out the sum for the books, buying the types and presses, thinking it would end the problem. The burning of the books also brought about the attention of the people, who thought that there must be something different in them that they would be so destroyed. And so, the demand for them increased.

Of course, what followed is expected, many were persecute; as was John Raimund, a Dutchman who was punished for causing the printing of fifteen hundred books to be printed at Antwerp and sending many to England. William Tyndale's brother John was punished for "sending five marks to his brother, and receiving letters from him;" and condemning Thomas Patmore and another merchant of London, "to do penance by riding to the standard in Cheapside, with their faces to their horses' tails, having the testaments hung thickly round them, fastened to their gowns; they were then compelled to cast the books into a fire kindled on purpose to consume them."[2]

---

[1] Fox's Book of Martyrs, Ibid, page 180.
[2] The Lives of the British Reformers, (Tyndale) page 6. Note: Each chapter in this book starts with page number one.

The works of Tyndale were numerous, one of which was a tract, "The Obedience of a Christian Man, and how Christian Rulers ought to govern;" of which an anecdote has been preserved: "Ann Boleyn, before she was queen, lent to Mrs. Gainsford, one of her female attendants, a tract written by Tindal, called, 'The Obedience of a Christian Man.' One day as she was reading it, a young gentleman named Zouch, also in the service of Lady Ann snatched the book away in sport, and refused to restore it. He was, however, induced to peruse the tract; and his heart was so affected by its contents, that 'he was never well but when he was reading that book.' Cardinal Wolsey had directed all the ecclesiastics about the court, to take especial care to prevent the writings of the reformers from being circulated there, lest they should come into the hands of the king; but this very caution proved the means of bringing to pass what he most feared! Dr. Sampson, the dean of the royal chapel, saw this book one day in the young man's hand, who was reading it in the chapel; most probably being weary of attendance upon the mass, the processions, and other mummeries. The dean called Zouch, and took the book from him, and gave it to the cardinal. Some days after, Lady Ann asked hr attendant for the book, who, 'on her knees, told all the circumstances,' doubtless being fearful lest her mistress, as well as herself, should come into trouble from this carelessness. Lady Ann instantly went to the king, and 'upon her knees' entreated his help, that the book might be restored. Henry interfered, and at his command the book was given up to Lady Ann, who brought it to him, requesting he should read it. The king did so, and was much pleased with the contents, saying, 'This book is for me and all kings to read.'"[1]

Tyndale was a true translator of the God's Word, the Scriptures, testifying, "I call God to record against the day we shall appear before our Lord Jesus, to give a reckoning of our doings, that I never altered one syllable of God's word against my conscience, nor would do this day, if all that is in earth, whether it be honour, pleasure, or riches, might be given me."

William Tyndale had a very trusting nature as well as a loving one as he visited the poor and needy, giving to them as he was able. However the bishops and Sir Thomas More were not so trusting, being more devious, and so studied Tyndale and his nature that they might stop him in his teaching and writing. Tyndale had been residing in the home of Thomas Pointz, who kept a house of English merchants. Out of England came a true deceiver, one Henry Philips. Philips developed an acquaintance with Tyndale, to the point that he was invited to the lodging

---

[1] The Lives of the British Reformers, ibid, page 12.

of Tyndale and shown his study and books. Philips soon went to the town of Barrois, eighteen miles from Antwerp. Returning to the lodging of Tyndale he asked for the whereabouts of Tyndale. He had brought officers with him in order to detain him. When he saw Tyndale he invited him to dine with him and the trap was set. At dinner time Tyndale set forth with Philips. There was a long narrow entry to Pointz's house where two could not go side by side. Philips urged Tyndale to go first and, as he had set offices at the door, he pointed his finger over Tyndale so that the officers knew who take to prison. The procurator-general took away the books and things which belonged to Tyndale.

William Tyndale remained in prison, where he refused an advocate saying that he would answer for himself. Although Tyndale did not deserve death, he was condemned by the emperor's decree. He was tied to the stake, strangled by the hangman, and consumed by fire, at the town of Vilvorde in 1536. From the stake Tyndale cried with a loud voice, "Lord! Open the king of England's eyes."

It is recorded of William Tyndale: "He was a man without spot, or blemish of rancour, or malice, full of mercy and compassion, so that no man living was able to reprove him of any king of sin or crime, although his righteousness and justification depended not thereupon before God, but only upon the blood of Christ, and his faith upon the same; in which faith he died with constancy at Filford, and now resteth with the glorious company of Christ's martyrs blessedly in the Lord, who be blessed in all his saints. Amen.

"And thus much of the life and story of the true servant and martyr of God, William Tindal, who for his notable pains and travail, may well be called the apostle of England in this our Later age."[1]

---

[1] The Lives of the British Reformers, ibid, page 14.

How is the word made effectual to salvation?

The Spirit of God maketh the reading, but especially the preaching of the word, and effectual means of enlightening, convincing, and humbling sinners; of driving them out of themselves, and drawing them unto Christ; of conforming them to his image, and subduing them to his will; of strengthening them against temptations and corruptions; of building them up in grace, and establishing their hearts in holiness and comfort through faith unto salvation.

-The Larger Catechism, Q & A 155

John Rogers
"That which I have preached I will seal with my blood"

John Rodgers was born at Deritend in the parish of Aston. He was educated at the University of Cambridge, graduating in 1526. For some years he was chosen and served as chaplain by the English Merchants adventurers at Antwerp in Brabant. At this time he fell in company with William Tyndale and Miles Coverdale, both of whom had to forsake their native country because of their love for the truth and baring the superstitions and idolatry of the Roman Church. Discussing the Scriptures with these men Rogers came to the knowledge of the gospel of God, casting off the they heavy yoke of popery, joining with them in "that most painful and profitable labour of translating the Bible into the English tongue, which is entitled, The Translation of Thomas Matthew."[1] Rogers also translated some homilies and other writings of Melancthon.

William Tyndale was arrested in the spring of 1535 and was executed and burned on October 6, 1536. We remember his last words to be "O Lord, open the king of England's eyes." John Marshall writes in his paper on Rogers: "God wonderfully answered the prayer of his dying servant and martyr. Henry's policy about an English Bible, no doubt under the power of God; changed, and Thomas Cromwell was able to persuade his sovereign to license the Matthew Bible. It is generally considered that the name Thomas Matthew not only concealed the name of John Rogers, but more significantly, the name of William Tyndale. At the end of the whole Old Testament there are the large letters, 'W.T.'.[2]

Faithfully serving the Lord under the reign of king Edward, who banished popery out of England, Rogers preached the Gospel fervently. Nicholas Ridley, bishop of London gave him a prebend[3] in the Cathedral Church of St. Paul. The dean chose him to be the reader of the divinity lecture there. Rogers diligently served the Lord until the time when queen Mary obtained the crown, and banished the true religion, "and brought in the antichrist of Rome, with his idolatry and superstition." When the Queen came to the tower of London in August of 1553, Rogers was

---

[1] The Lives of the British Reformers, ibid, *The Life, Admonition, and Martyrdom of John Rogers*, page 294; with this footnote: "This was the second printed edition of the English Bible; it was edited by Coverdale, assisted by Rogers, and was sanctioned by royal authority. The New Testament, and the first half of the Old, were from Tindal's version, the remainder from Coverdale's.)

[2] John E. Marshall Life and Writings, John J. Murray, The Banner of Truth Trust, Edinburgh, 2005, page 93.

[3] "The stipend or maintenance granted out of the estate of a cathedral or collegiate church. Prebends are *simple* or *dignitary*; *simple*, when they are restricted to the revenue only, and *dignitary*, when they have jurisdiction annexed to them." –Noah Webster's Dictionary 1828

called upon to give a sermon at St. Paul's cross. He confirmed the truth, holing fast the true doctrines of Scripture as he and others had during the time of king Edward. He exhorted the people to be faithful and to beware of the idolatry and superstition of the popery. The council, being overcome by the popish bishops, called Rogers to account for his sermon. He gave a wise and godly answer, and was dismissed. The Queen set forth a proclamation that prohibited such preaching, and Rogers was called again before the council.

John Marshall titled his paper on Rogers: "John Rogers: Proto-Martyr of the English Reformation." His introduction reads: "It is Monday, 4 February 1555, and Mary Tudor, commonly known as 'Bloody Mary', is on the throne. The French Ambassador, Count Noailles, sends a report to his sovereign back in Paris, informing him of the situation in London. 'This day was performed the confirmation of the alliance between the Pope and this kingdom, by the public and solemn sacrifice of a preaching doctor named Rogers, who has been burned alive for being a Lutheran; but he died persisting in his opinion. At this conduct the greatest part of the people took such pleasure that they were not afraid to make him many exclamations to strengthen his courage. Even his children assisted at it, comforting him in such a manner that it seemed as if he had been led to a wedding.'

Thus died the proto-martyr of the English Reformation. Two hundred and eighty-two men and women were consequently put to death as Mary sought to burn our Protestantism from her realm. At the stake Rogers was offered a pardon if he would recant, but he would have parley with error, nor buy his life by selling the truth. He would seal with his blood the message he delighted to preach."[1]

For a long time Rogers remained in his own house as a prisoner. Bonner, bishop of London, could not put up with such an honest neighbor, so Rogers was removed to the Newgate prison, where he was lodged with thieves and murderers. He was questioned by the authorities. Rogers wrote this testimony of his examination, "I have a true spirit, quoth I, agreeing and obeying the word of God; and would further have said, that I was never the worse, but the better to be earnest in a just true cause, and in my Master Christ's matters; but I could not be heard." And in closing wrote, "To be short, he (the lord chancellor) read my condemnation before me, particularly mentioning therein but two articles; first, that I affirmed the Romish catholic church to be the church of antichrist; and that I denied the reality of their sacraments. He caused me to be degraded and condemned, and put into the hands of the laity,

---

[1] John E. Marshall Life and Writings, ibid, pages 89-90.

and so he gave me over into the sheriff's hands, which were much better than his."

Rogers was taken out of Newgate prison and delivered to Smithfield the place of execution. As Rogers was led to the place of his execution his wife and children met him; his children being eleven in number with one sucking on her breast. Thus the time came for his death and the truth of his words: "That which I have preached I will seal with my blood;" which was his answer to sheriff Woodroof's question he would revoke his abominable doctrine and his evil opinions of the sacrament of the altar. Rogers was asked again, before his burning at the stake, if he would recant, to which he absolutely refused. "He was the first Martyr of all the blessed company that suffered in queen Mary's time; he gave the first adventure upon the fire."[1]

Psalm 93[2]

The Lord doth reign, and cloth'd is he with majesty most bright;
His works do shew him cloth'd to be, and girt about with might.
The world is also established, that it cannot depart.
Thy throne is fix'd of old, and thou from everlasting art.

The floods, O Lord, have lifted up, they lifted up their voice;
The floods have lifted up their waves, and made a mighty noise.
But yet the Lord, that is on high, is more of might by far
Than noise of many waters is, or great sea-billows are.

Thy testimonies ev'ry one is faithfulness excel;
And holiness for ever, Lord, thine house becometh well.

[1] The Lives of the British Reformers, ibid, page 31.
[2] The Comprehensive Psalter, Scottish Metrical Version with Music, Blue Banner Books, Rowlett, Texas, 2000, page 205.

Psalm CXIX
[A good prayer for each morning]

Blessed are the undefiled in the way; who walk in the Law of the Lord. Blessed are they that keep his testimonies; and that seek him with the whole heart. They also do no iniquities; they walk in his ways. Thou hast commanded us to keep thy precepts diligently. O that my ways were directed to keep thy statutes! Then shall I not be ashamed when I have respect unto all thy commandments. I will praise thee with uprightness of heart; when I shall have learned thy righteous judgments. I will keep thy statutes; O forsake me not utterly.

Psalm 119:1-8

The Scriptures

The wicked take counsel against Christ the King, venting their anger against His Word and His Church. The true Church reveals its obedience to the Lord in their obedience to His Word.[1] Scripture is not a book about God but a Book written by God. "All scripture is given by inspiration of God, and is profitable for doctrine, for reproof, for correction, for instruction in righteousness" [2 Tim. 3:16]. The Confession teaches that "it pleased the Lord, at sundry times, and in divers manners, to reveal Himself, and to declare His will unto His Church; and afterwards, for the better preserving an propagating of the truth, and or the more sure establishment and comfort of the Church against the corruption of the flesh, and the malice of Satan, and of the world, to commit the same wholly unto writing; which maketh the Holy Scripture to be most necessary."[2]

Paul identifies the Church as "the house of God, which is the church of the living God, the pillar and ground of truth" [1Tim. 3:15]. The Triune Creator of heaven and earth has unveiled for His people the reality of all things, including faith and life. The Scripture "principally teach, what man is to believe, concerning God, and what duty God requires of man;" and "by their light and power to convince and convert sinners, to comfort and build up believers unto salvation; but the Spirit of God bearing witness by and with the scriptures in the heart of man, is alone able fully to persuade it that they are the very word of God."[3]

From generation to generation the Church of our Lord has sought to be faithful in their obedience to His Word. The world seeks to destroy that Word, as they have in generations past: "By countless wondrous means Satan with the whole world has tried either oppress it or overturn it,[4] to obscure and obliterate in utterly from the memory of men—yet, like the palm, it has risen ever higher and has remained unassailable. Indeed, there has scarcely ever been either sophist or rhetorician of superior ability who did not try his power against it, yet all were unsuccessful. Such facts as these should be accounted of no slight

---

[1] "Blessed is the man that walketh not in the counsel of the ungodly, not standeth in the way of sinners, nor sitteth in the seat of the scornful. But his delight is in the law of the Lord; and in his law doth he meditate day and night" [Psalm 1:1-2].

[2] Westminster Confession of Faith, Free Presbyterian Publications, Glasgow, 2001, *Of the Holy Scripture*, pages 19-20.

[3] Ibid, LARGER CATECHISM, Q & A's 5 & 4, pages 130-131.

[4] For example, in America, the ACLU desires to eliminate Christianity from all public life.

importance. The whole power of earth has armed itself to destroy it, yet these efforts have gone up in smoke."[1]

Many believe that the Scripture has been inspired by God, but only in the Autographs (the original writings) can we claim a truly inerrant and infallible Bible. The belief that only the Autographs can be declared to be inerrant, leads men to the doctrine or teaching that the Westminster Confession must be reinterpreted; which leads men to continually publish new translations of the Bible. They become Bible-Archaeologists, digging into manuscripts and writings of men in the hope that they will be able to reconstruct the original text.

However, The Confession teaches appropriately, that the writing of the Old and New Testaments, "being immediately inspired by God, and by His singular care and providence kept pure in all ages, are therefore authentical; so as, in all controversies of religion, the Church is finally to appeal unto them. But, because these original tongues are not known to all the people of God, who have right unto, and interest in the Scriptures, and are commanded, in the fear of God, to read and search them, therefore they are to be translated into the vulgar language of every nation unto which they come, that the Word of God dwelling plentifully in all, they may worship Him in an acceptable manner; and, through patience and comfort of the Scriptures may have hope."[2]

Scripture attests to the truth that the words which God inspired are efficacious in and of itself. The Psalmist wrote, by inspiration, "Thy testimonies are wonderful; therefore doth my soul keep them. The entrance of thy words giveth light; it giveth understanding unto the simple" [Ps. 119:129-130]. If God did not preserve His 'words'—inspired in the original—providentially cared for and preserved from generation to generation, then by what authority do we say this word is good and another is not? Or, how could our Savior say with authority, that what has been written by the prophets by inspiration of the Spirit, can be searched and believed: "Search the Scriptures; for in them ye think ye have eternal life; and they are they which testify of me," and, "For had ye believed Moses, ye would have believed me; for he wrote of me. But if ye believe not his writings, how shall ye believe my words" [John 5:39, 46-47]?

The Westminster Assembly attests to the "infallible rule of faith and practice" as they looked at Scriptures to rule their deliberations, rather than those who seek out proof from a Bible which only contains the

[1] John Calvin, Institutes of the Christian Religion, The Westminster Press, Philadelphia, 1973, Book I, Ch. VIII, 12, page 91.
[2] Westminster Confession of Faith, Free Presbyterian Publications, ibid, Ch. 1, *Of the Holy Scripture*, pages 23-24.

word of God. This Convocation of divines sought to unify the Church of our Lord Jesus Christ by firmly relying on the Scriptures as the Word of God. For and example, Dr. Symington, in a lecture on the Assembly, quotes Robert Baillie of Glasgow as to their dependency on Scripture: "Every committee, as the Parliament gives order in write to take any purposes to consideration, takes a portion, and in their afternoon meeting prepares matters for the assembly, sets down their mind in distinct propositions, backs their propositions with texts of Scripture. After the prayer, Mr. Byfield, the scribe, reads the proposition and scriptures, whereupon the Assembly debates in a most grave and orderly way."[1] The Church today needs to understand the place of Scripture in their deliberations. The weakness of many a debate is a fragile view of Scripture. Decisions are sometimes made on expediency, human practicality, former practices, or false propositions. This weakness is revealed in the formation of committees upon which both sides of the issue are represented; which leads to a consensus of opinion rather than a Biblical understanding of what is true. It would be better to have each side present a paper that will lead an assembly to discuss or debate on Scriptural grounds. To do so the Church must have an understanding that the Writer of Scripture has preserved His Word.

The Martyrs attest to the doctrines of the Word of God, that they are true, and worthy to be obeyed unto death. They claimed the Word to be supreme authority over all areas of life, family, church, and civil governments; in the Church: doctrine, government, and worship. John Calvin wrote in his *Institutes* of the strength of the martyrs, *Martyrs died for the Scripture doctrine*: "Now with what assurance ought we to enlist under that doctrine which we see confirmed and attested by the blood of so many holy men! They, having once received it, did not hesitate, courageously and intrepidly, and even with great eagerness, to suffer death for it. Should we not accept with sure and unshaken conviction what has been handed on to us with such a pledge? It is no moderate approbation of Scripture that it has been sealed by the blood of so many witnesses, especially when we reflect that they died to render testimony to the faith; not with fanatic excess (as erring spirits are sometimes accustomed to do), but with a firm and constant, yet sober, zeal toward God."[2]

Those who were sent to dungeon or stake stood with Luther as he held the Book firmly and said "Here I stand!" It was the Book they held in their hands, whose words were written upon their hearts and zealously

---

[1] Historical Sketch of The Westminster Assembly of Divines, William Symington, D.D., Presbyterian's Armoury Publications, 2002, page 24.
[2] Calvin: Institutes of the Christian Religion, ibid, Bk. 1, Ch. 18, page 92.

preached in houses and fields. They were not ignorant of the Word, but with it followed their Savior and King. "They furnished their persecutors with sufficient reasons for the part which they acted in opposing their wishes, and often so confounded their opponents in argument that they had not a word to say; and this was done, not merely by the more learned of their party,—gentlemen and ministers,—but frequently also by the illiterate peasants, who were dragged from the plough or the workshop, or from following the flocks on the heath. Let any one read the account of their examination before the Privy Council, or the statement of their principles given in the 'Cloud of Witnesses,' and say if they were uninstructed persons or men of weak minds, who could not give a reason of the hope that was in them."[1] It was the Word of God that gave them knowledge and understanding to protest against the tyranny of the state and the false teachings in the Church, contending "for the supremacy of the Lord Jesus Christ in his Church, a prerogative which the ruler of the nation impiously sought to arrogate to himself." In other words, they made excellent use of God's Scriptures. "They were 'the men of their counsel,' as David expresses it, and by their constant reading of the Bible they acquired more understanding than all their rulers. The word of God was their constant companion; and wherever they reposed, in the caves, or among the brown heath, or on the green hill-side, they had recourse to the oracles of truth for strength and comfort in their manifold perils. Great indeed was the power and sweetness of this word to them. They read every portion of it as if it had been spoken to them immediately by the mouth of God. It was the pasture on which they fed, and it was pleasant to their taste."[2]

Can you imagine these worthy saints taking up a book with eight different translations and, being fed thereby, crying out, Here I stand? Does truth come from a Bible study where each one gives an opinion and then the leader tries to bring it all together? Is not the Holy Spirit the Teacher and the children of God the disciples who sit at the feet of Jesus? Truth is not a fleeting fancy whereby the fool says 'I absolutely know there are no absolutes.'

Calvinism has a love for truth and for learning. The Great Commission is not given to fill the pews but to fill the heart and life of people with the Truth that sets them free. The Bible may not be a text book on all the aspects of science, but it is a book which teaches the truth of God's Creation, by which science must be tested. Truth was what the Calvinist sought after in all areas of education. "Wherever

---

[1] Traditions of the Covenanters, Rev. Robert Simpson, Presbyterian Board of Publication, Philadelphia, pages 125-126.
[2] Ibid, page 127.

Calvinism has gone, there knowledge and learning have been encouraged and there a sturdy race of thinkers has been trained. Calvinists have been the builders of great cathedrals, but they have been the builders of schools, colleges, and universities. When the Puritans from England, the Covenanters from Scotland, and the Reformed from Holland and Germany, came to America they brought with them not only the Bible and the Westminster Confession but also the school. And that is why our American Calvinism never

> 'Dreads the skeptic's puny hands,
> While near her school the church spire stands,
> Nor fears the blinded bigot's rule,
> While near her church spire stands a school.'"[1]

The Bible, the Scripture of the Old and New Testaments, is, in its proper sense, an historical account of the battle between Christ the King of righteousness and the ungodly that are of their father, Satan. The Martyrs fell to the sword of the ungodly because of their loyalty to Christ and His Word. "Recant! and become one with us, and we will give you life!" is the battle cry of the ungodly. Not only do the ungodly want Christians to keep to their pews, but they are to accept their authority within what they believe to be their world.

The Scriptures, the Word of God, is the foundation on which we stand. God has spoken to us about Himself and His Creation. The Word written is God's written history, sufficient and efficacious to give us all we need to know about God and ourselves. The Larger Catechism teaches us this truth: "The scriptures principally teach, what man is to believe concerning God, and what duty God requires of man.—The Scriptures make known what God is, the persons in the Godhead, his decrees, and the execution of his decrees." Paul sets our eyes upon the Word of God as that which has been given to the Church: "For whatsoever things were written aforetime were written for our learning; that we, through patience and comfort of the scriptures, might have hope" [Rom. 15:4]. Plus, we have the promise of our Savior that the Holy Spirit will be with us as the teacher of truth: "Howbeit when he, the Spirit of truth is come, he will guide you into all truth; for he shall not speak of himself; but whatsoever he shall hear, that shall he speak; and he shall show you things to come" [John 16:13]. For the truth we find in the Word is that of the Triune God, to His glory and our good.

To the glory of God the Geneva Bible is seeing a reformation. This translation of God's Word is being used by more and more of God's people. In the fourth edition of The Geneva Bible, *a facsimile of the 1599*

---

[1] The Reformed Doctrine of Predestination, Loraine Boettner, The Presbyterian and Reformed Publishing Company, Phillipsburg, N.J., 1979, pages 396-397.

edition printed by L. L. Brown Publishing. Michael Brown wrote that "Today most of those who consider themselves Calvanists have never heard of a Geneva Bible. A completely annotated Geneva Bible—with all the marginal notes of John Calvin, John Knox, and the other Reformers—has not been printed since 1644. This edition is the first completely annotated version since then," Brown continues with this interesting note: "Be careful when attempting to interpret marginal notes. In the 16th century the Bible was not just a spiritual guide, it was a legal document. The word 'argument' used before the chapters is even used today by attorneys on motions and briefs. This is further illustrated by the admonishment to study and obey God's statutes and judgments. There are no statutes in the New Testament (God's statutes are found in Exodus 20 to the end of Deuteronomy in the Old Testament), indicating a serious difference of opinion with today's 'God's Law is put away in Christ' crowd."

The Geneva Bible is being restored by Tolle Lege Press (web site, 1599genevabible.com); to be completed by the end of October or in November. Dr. Marshall Foster[1] begins his Introduction to the 1599 Geneva Bible: "The Geneva Bible has been the lost treasure of Christendom for almost 400 years. Nearly forgotten by the modern world, this version of the Holy Scriptures was translated and compiled by exiled reformers in Geneva (1557-1560) and stands alone in history as the force that transformed the English speaking world from the backwater of history to the center of civilization. The 2006 edition is the first completely new publication of the Geneva Bible available in modern times. This Bible is going to press at the exact year that America is celebrating its 400 Birthday with the settlement of Jamestown. As the cornerstone of the American experiment, the Geneva Bible was surely aboard the three ships that sailed from England to Virginia in December of 1606. The famous New England Pilgrims relied on the Geneva Bible for comfort and strength on their 66 day voyage aboard the Mayflower in1620, and needed its insights as they wrote the Mayflower Compact, the first compact constitutional government in history."

Dr. Gary DeMar[2] wrote an article titled, The Forgotten Translation, which refers to the history of the Geneva Bible: "When Mary Tudor (Bloody Mary) became queen of England in 1553, she was determined to roll back the Reformation and reinstate Roman Catholicism. Mary had strong ties to

---

[1] Dr. Marshall Foster is the President of the Mayflower Institute & Member of the 1599 Geneva Bible Advisory Board.

[2] Gary DeMar is President of American Vision & Honorary Member of the 1599 Geneva Bible Advisory Board. This is a portion of his article from the web site of American Vision, americanvision.org. This should also remind us that God preserves His Scriptures from generation to generation.

Catholic Spain. She married Philip II of Spain and induced the English Parliament to recognize the authority of papal Rome. Mary met with a great deal of resistance from Protestant reformers in her own country. Mary showed no signs of compromise. The persecution of Protestants followed.

The era known as the Marian Exile drove hundreds of English scholars to the Continent with little hope of ever seeing their home and friends again. God used this exodus experience to advance the Reformation. A number of English Protestant divines settled in Calvin's Geneva: Miles Coverdale, John Foxe, Thomas Sampson, and William Whittingham. With the protection of the Genevan civil authorities and the support of John Calvin and the Scottish Reformer John Knox, the Church of Geneva determined to produce an English Bible without the need for the imprimatur of either England or Rome - the Geneva Bible.

Translation Work Begins In 1557

The Geneva translators produced a revised New Testament in English in 1557 that was essentially a revision of Tyndale's revised and corrected 1534 edition. Much of the work was done by William Whittingham, the brother-in-law of John Calvin. The Geneva New Testament was barely off the press when work began on a revision of the entire Bible, a process that took more than two years. The new translation was checked with Theodore Beza's earlier work and the Greek text. In 1560 a complete revised Bible was published, translated according to the Hebrew and Greek, and conferred with the best translations in divers languages, and dedicated to Queen Elizabeth I. After the death of Mary, Elizabeth was crowned queen in 1558, once again moving England toward Protestantism. The Geneva Bible was finally printed in England in 1575 only after the death of Archbishop Matthew Parker, editor of the Bishop's Bible.

England's Most Popular Bible

While other English translations failed to capture the hearts of the reading public, the Geneva Bible was instantly popular. Between 1560 and 1644 at least 144 editions appeared. For forty years after the publication of the King James Bible, the Geneva Bible continued to be the Bible of the home. Oliver Cromwell used extracts from the Geneva Bible for his Soldier's Pocket Bible which he issued to the army."

Grant, Almighty God, since we so travel through this world that our attention is easily arrested, and our judgment darkened, when we behold the power of the impious refulgent and terrible to ourselves and others: Grant, I say, that we may raise our eyes upwards, and consider how much power thou hast conferred upon thine only-begotten Son. Grant, also, that he may rule and govern us by the might of his Spirit, protect us by his faithfulness and guardianship, and compel the whole world to promote our salvation; thus may we rest calmly under his protection, and fight with that boldness and patience which he both commands and commends, until at length we enjoy the fruit of the victory which thou hast promised, and which thou wilt provide for us in thy heavenly kingdom.–Amen.

–John Calvin, (Daniel Commentary)

Victory in Suffering and Persecution

The Christian does not stand alone, but is a citizen-servant in the Kingdom of the Son of God, the King of kings. St. Augustine wrote of this Kingdom as "The City of God." Augustine, called it a "glorious city of God," introducing his work in these words, "I have undertaken its defense against those who prefer their own gods to the Founder of this city, a city surpassingly glorious, whether we view it as it still lives by faith in this fleeting course of time, and sojourns as a stranger in the midst of the ungodly, or as it shall dwell in the fixed stability of its eternal seat, which it now with patience waits for, expecting until 'righteousness shall return unto judgment.' And it obtains, by virtue of its excellence, final victory and perfect peace."

Those who prefer their own gods are adversaries and enemies of Christ. The Martyrs are those who are faithful citizens of this holy Tabernacle, the City of God on earth. The prophet of the glorious Lord who "is our judge, the Lord is our lawgiver, the Lord is our king; he will save us;" and He has made to His own this promise, "Look upon Zion, the city of our solemnities; thine eyes shall see Jerusalem a quiet habitation, a tabernacle that shall not be removed, neither shall any of the cords be broken" [Isaiah 33:20-22].

John Bunyan gives the name 'Mansoul' to God's City in his discourse on "The Holy War." Truly, both the soul of each child of God and the soul of the Kingdom of the divine Prince are in the sights of the ungodly, whose singular desire is for their destruction. The ungodly set themselves up as the princes of this world, whose authority must be obeyed. They tear down the righteous and moral law of the true Prince and Ruler, making war against His redeemed subjects. Bunyan, in his allegory, has a representative of Diabolus coming to the city of Mansoul by the name of Captain Sepulchre, saying, "O ye inhabitants of the rebellious town of Mansoul! I summon you, in the name of the prince Diabolus, that without any more ado you set open the gates of your town and admit the great lord to come in. But if you shall still rebel, when we have taken to us the town by force we will swallow you up as the grave. Wherefore if you hearken to my summons, says so, and if not, then let me know." Captain Sepulchre, after reminding them that they once followed Diabolus, lying as did the deceiving serpent, that Emmanuel had lost the right to call them back to himself, he continues, "If thou shalt quietly yield up thyself, then our old friendship shall be renewed; but if thou shalt yet refuse and rebel, then expect nothing but fire and sword."[1]

---

[1] John Bunyan, <u>The Complete Works of</u>, Bradley, Garretson & Co., Philadelphia, 1874, *The Holy* War, page 451.

Truly, Christians are rebellious, refusing to return to the city of destruction. The world continues its assault, urging them to recant and return. However, we now belong to Christ the King! For "Thus saith the Lord; I am returned unto Zion, and will dwell in the midst of Jerusalem; and Jerusalem shall be called a city of truth; and the mountain of the Lord of hosts the holy mountain" [Zech. 8:3]. We have a majestic Prince to follow and obey, one who has given us a command to make disciples of all nations by His authority, strength, and truth [Matt. 28:18-20]. Yes, there will be persecution: "The kings of the earth set themselves, and the rulers take counsel together, against the Lord, and against his anointed, saying, Let us break their bands asunder, and cast away their cords from us" [Ps. 2:2-3]. The Lord warns His disciples, "If the world hate you, ye know that it hated me before it hated you. If ye were of the world, the world would love his own; but because ye are not of the world, but I have chosen you out of the world, therefore the world hateth you. Remember the word that I said unto you. The servant is not greater than his lord. If they have persecuted me, they will also persecute you" [John 15:18-20].

The warning about the reality of persecution is given by our Lord to encourage our faith. Discouragement is for the wicked not for the righteous. For our "God who commanded the light to shine out of darkness, hath shined in our hearts, to give the light of the knowledge of the glory of God in the face of Jesus Christ. For we have this treasure in earthen vessels, that the excellency of the power may be of God, and not of us. We are troubled on every side, yet not distressed; we are perplexed, but not in despair; persecuted, but not forsaken; cast down, but not destroyed; always bearing about in the body the dying of the Lord Jesus that the life also of Jesus might be made manifest in our body. For we which live are always delivered unto death for Jesus' sake, that the life also of Jesus might be made manifest in our mortal flesh" [2 Cor. 4:6-11]. Surely there were and will be those who face "trial of cruel mockings and scourgings, yea, moreover of bonds and imprisonment; they were stoned, they were sawn asunder, were tempted, were slain with the sword; they wandered about in sheepskins and goatskins; being destitute, afflicted, tormented; (of whom the world was not worthy;) they wandered in deserts, and in mountains, and in dens and caves of the earth" [Heb. 11:36-38].

Victory is promised in the Word of God. Christ's Church, His Kingdom on earth, is one that will face suffering with the hope of victory. On the Isle of Patmos the beloved apostle John saw Satan cast out into the earth, his wrath is heard but his end is death. John heard a loud voice from heaven, saying, "Now is come salvation, and strength, and the kingdom of our God, and the power of his Christ; for the accuser of our brethren is cast down, which accused them before our God day and night. And they overcame him by the blood of the Lamb, and by the word of their testimony; and they loved not their lives unto the death" [Rev. 12:9-11].

The Kingdom of our Lord has come. The reign of the Son of God, Christ Jesus (Joshua=Jehovah is salvation) is the reigning Sovereign today. The angel Gabriel was sent by the Triune God to Mary, and spoke of the son to be born, "He shall be great, and shall be called the Son of the Highest; and the Lord God shall give unto him the throne of his father David; and he shall reign over the house of Jacob forever; and of his kingdom there shall be no end" [Luke 1:32-33]. The deceiver and accuser has been cast down and the kingdom is here as promised: "But if I cast out devils by the Spirit of God, then the kingdom of God is come unto you" [Matt. 12:28].

The Church of the Lord Jesus is a conquering Church. This is particularly revealed in the birth, life, death, resurrection, and ascension of Christ Jesus; summarized in Revelation 12:5, "And she brought forth a man child, who was to rule all nations with a rod of iron; and her child was caught up unto God, and to his throne." The incarnation of Emmanuel (God with us) culminates in His ascension to the eternal throne as King of kings. He was anointed King of kings and Lord of lords. Thus Christ fulfilled the covenant promise; i.e., "Yet have I set my king upon my holy hill of Zion. I will declare the decree: the Lord hath said to me, Thou art my Son; this day have I begotten thee. Ask of me, and I shall give thee the heathen for thine inheritance, and the uttermost parts of the earth for thy possession. Thou shalt break them with a rod of iron; thou shalt dash them in pieces like a potter's vessel" [Ps. 2:6-9]. Therefore the nations, its kings, judges, and rulers are to honor the Son; they are to "Serve the Lord with fear, and rejoice with trembling" [2:11].

However, the ungodly still seek to do war with the King of kings and His Church. Thus the Christian martyrs do not die for a cause but for the King. And the armor they carry is His Book. But we do not have a faith-unto-death that acknowledges defeat. We understand that there will be victory. The vision of the birth of Christ illustrates the great victory of our Savior by revealing a great red dragon who "stood before the woman which was ready to be delivered, for to devour the child as soon as it was born" [Rev. 12:4]. Dr. Nigel Lee[1] gives us this picture of the birth of Christ, "Satan's futile attempt to destroy the infant Jesus soon after He was born —predictably ended in utter failure. For the woman, the Older

---

[1] The Works of Rev. Prof. Dr. F.N. Lee, web site: dr-fnlee.org, PDF *John's Revelation Unveiled.*

Testament's Church, through the agency of the blessed virgin Mary as a Member of that Church, brought forth a male child alias a baby boy in the person of the infant Jesus. Not only was the then-tiny Jesus not destroyed by wicked Herod as Rome's Puppet-King. Too, many also in Israel even then confessed His Lordship. And three important leaders also from the East even then acknowledged Him as their King, too."

We also are encouraged to see the Church-Triumphant in the *war in heaven*: "And there was war in heaven: Michael and his angels fought against the dragon; and the dragon fought and his angels, and prevailed not; neither was their place found any more in heaven. And the great dragon was cast out, that old serpent, called the Devil, and Satan, which deceiveth the whole world; he was cast out into the earth, and his angels were cast out with him" [Rev. 12:7-9]. Satan and his angels have been defeated; while Christ ascended in victory and sits at the right hand of His heavenly Father, "where as the Son of man He started to reign, and whence He reigns for evermore, and keeps on ruling throughout His Cosmos" (N. Lee).

Persecution comes, not because we have been faithful, but that our King is faithful. His reign has begun: "The kingdoms of this world are become *the kingdoms* of our Lord, and of his Christ; and he shall reign forever and ever" [Rev. 11:15]. Sing out today: "Worthy is the Lamb that was slain, to receive power and riches and wisdom and strength, and honor and glory and blessing!" [Rev. 5:12].

No, O Emmanuel!
We shall not be guilty of tarnishing the honour of thy glorious name.
We rejoice in thy boundless dominion,
and unhesitatingly proclaim thee Lord of all!

… When assailed by Satanic temptations, it must matter of joyful reflection to the people of God, to know that Christ has dominion over infernal spirits, and can limit and restrain, and overrule for good, all their operations; that they can have no power over these except as it is given by him; that the power they possess is entirely under his control; and that he possesses the right and the ability, as he stands pledged, to destroy in the end all the works of the devil.

--William Symington, Messiah the Prince

The Songs of the Church are the Psalms of God's Word

The following theses' are part of
>"A series of convention papers bearing
>upon the place of the Psalms in
>the worship of the Church."

Included in the 'Preface' are these words of purpose:
' "Under the direction of the General Assembly of the United Presbyterian Church of North America two conventions were held in the autumn of 1905, the first in Pittsburgh and the second in Chicago, to promote the claims of the Psalms in the field of worship. . . .The Psalter, composed under the inspirations of the Holy Spirit, is the common possession of the whole family of God, its ordained manual of praise. It is the oldest hymn-book in existence, have a connected record through thousands of years down to our own times, and it is consecrated forever as having been the hymnary of our Saviour and of the Apostolic Church."[1]

---

[1] The Psalms in Worship, The United Presbyterian Board of Publications, Pittsburgh, Pa., 1907, page 5.

THE SINGING OF PRAISE A DUTY[1]
By President F. M. Spencer, D. D., Sterling, Kansas

That singing praise to God is a duty can be established by a fivefold argument.

First. It is taught by the light of nature and reason. Man is made for song. The vocal organs are fashioned for the production of melodious sounds. The voice as a musical instrument is more perfect than any made by man. It is susceptible of finer modulations and more exquisite renderings. These sounds are conveyed to the tympanum of the ear in all their richness and sweetness, and are perceived and interpreted by the mind. It is natural for man to sing, to give expression to his sentiments, his feelings, and his convictions in song. Love is not slow in seizing upon this vehicle for giving expression to her finest and tenderest emotions. Patriotism, too, is not unmindful of this means of arousing the minds of men, stirring them to their depths, and exciting them to deeds of heroism. How natural, then, that the deepest and strongest emotions of the soul, flowing out in gratitude and love, should be expressed in vocal and exultant praise? This argument is strengthened by the fact that service of song is not confined to this life nor to the human race. In the Revelation, chp. xiv., we are told that the one hundred and forty-four thousand sang a new song before the throne; and when the angelic host came down at the birth of Jesus they sang: "Glory to God in the highest, and on earth peace, good will toward men."

Second. It is a commanded duty. It is not necessary to quote more than a tithe of the many express passages commanding us to sing praise to God. A few are given. "Sing unto the Lord, O ye saints of His, and give thanks at the remembrance of His holiness." Ps. xxx. 4. "Sing praises to God, sing praises unto our King, sing praises. For God is the King of all the earth: sing ye praises with understanding." Ps. xlvii. 6, 7. "Make a joyful noise unto God, all ye lands: Sing forth the honor of His name; make His praise glorious." Ps. lxvi. 1, 2. "Sing aloud unto God our strength: make a joyful noise unto the God of Jacob." Ps. lxxxi. 1. "Make a joyful noise unto the Lord, all ye lands. Serve the Lord with gladness: come before his presence with singing." Ps. c. 1, 2. Many of the one hundred and fifty Psalms begin with the short, terse, expressive, "Praise ye the Lord." Frequently this is followed by a command to sing His praises, as in Ps. cxlix. 1: "Praise ye the Lord. Sing unto the Lord a new song, and His praise in the congregation of saints."

---

[1] The Psalms in Worship, ibid, pages 39-43.

No command is more frequently and emphatically imposed upon God's people in the Old Testament than is the duty of singing praise to God. In the New Testament these commands are renewed and made emphatic. Paul writing to the Colossians (iii. 16) says: "Let the word of Christ dwell in you richly in all wisdom; teaching and admonishing one another in psalms and hymns and spiritual songs, singing with grace in your hearts to the Lord." In Ephesians, v. 18, 19, he says: "Be filled with the Spirit; speaking to yourselves in psalms and hymns and spiritual songs, singing and making melody in your heart to the Lord." Language in the form of a command could not insist more clearly and distinctly upon the duty of singing praise to God.

Third. This duty is taught by approved examples. The first notable example of this is recorded in Ex. xv. When God had brought Israel out of Egypt, and across the Red Sea in safety, "Then sang Moses and the children of Israel this song unto the Lord: I will sing unto the Lord, for He hath triumphed gloriously: the horse and his rider hath He thrown into the des." Miriam, the prophetess, and the women who followed her answered with the same song: "Sing ye to the Lord, for He hath triumphed gloriously; the horse and his rider hath He thrown into the sea." In the days of David we find appointed in the Church singers who were to preside over and lead this part of the public worship. This service must have been in the tabernacle in the time of David. In the time of Solomon it was in the temple. The same service was continued in the time of Ezra: "And they sang together by course in praising and giving thanks unto the Lord; because He is good, for His mercy endureth forever toward Israel."

Our Saviour and His disciples sang an hymn, generally supposed to have been the Hallel, Pss. cxiii.-cxviii., just after the institution of the Lord's Supper. When Paul and Silas were doing mission work at Philippi they were arrested, beaten, cast into prison, thrust into the inner dungeon, and their feet made fast in the stocks. There they prayed and sang praises to God at the midnight hour till the prisoners heard them and God Himself shook the building with an earthquake, opened the doors, and released the prisoners. Thus God has given His seal to the example of those who, in both dispensations, have sung praises to His name.

Fourth. Singing His praise glorifies God. If it be true that "man's chief end is to glorify God," then singing praise to Him is a duty. This argument has special reference to the use of inspired songs. Human compositions are largely subjective. David said, "I have set the Lord always before me." The Psalms are objective in that from first to last

God is set before the mind. His perfections are the theme. His work is the subject. His glory is the end.

The Psalms are an epitome of the whole Bible. In the Second Psalm the Father and Son are presented, and in the Fifty-First the Holy Spirit. Thus we have the doctrine of the Trinity. In the Psalms God is the Creator and Preserver of all things: "In wisdom hast Thou made them all." "Lord, Thou preservest man and beast."

The Psalms are full of Christ. In the Fortieth Psalm He gives Himself to the work of man's redemption: "Lo, I come: in the volume of the book it is written of Me, I delight to do Thy will, O my God." In the Twenty-Second Psalm His sufferings are described and there is given His language upon the Cross: "My God, My God, why hast Thou forsaken me?" In the Sixty-Eighth Psalm we have the glory of His ascension. He it is Who ascends on high leading captivity captive, and receiving gifts for men. Christ is the perfect man of the First Psalm, the shepherd of the Twenty-Third, the bridegroom of the Forty-Fifth, the rock of the Fortieth, and the King of Glory of the Twenty-Fourth. There are no other compositions which in such a transcendent way exhibit the divine perfections, and since God knows just what He wishes us to sing, and has given us the songs to be sung, it follows that we glorify Him when we in song make known to the world His praise.

Fifth. Singing praise to God has a helpful subjective influence. Music has in itself a helpful, soul-stirring, uplifting power. God has planned not only that we shall glorify Him, but also that we shall enjoy Him. In no selfish spirit does He ask us to sing His praise. We are to sing in order that we may obtain a blessing. Ten thousand times ten thousand can bear witness to this truth. God's Word is sung into people. The singing seems to open the gates of the soul till it is flooded with joy. It is not possible to sing "with the spirit and the understanding" the words which God has given to be sung without being wafted heavenward. The singing of God's songs tends to purify the soul, to strengthen the intellect, and to form Godlike character. If they who from the cradle to the grave sin the songs which God has given to be sung should be found zealous for purity, in His worship, conscientious in the observance of His day, self-sacrificing in mission work, and loyal to Christ as King of nations, all the praise should be given to Him who planned the service of song.

Corollary I. The praise service should not be crowed out of the worship at the family altar. It is not true that there is no time for this service. We cannot afford to give it up in order to find a little more time to get gain or pleasure.

Corollary II. The praise service can be improved in most of our congregations. In the mad haste for new books and new tunes many are unable to sing at all. Before the tune is half learned it may be discarded. The tendency is to minify the words and magnify the music. When the whole attention and thought must be given to the music in order to sing at all we sing by rote and scarcely know what we sing. The music gets ninety-nine parts of our attention and the sentiment one lone part. This evil will be corrected when we settle down to one good tune to each Psalm or part of a Psalm. Then we will leave a little time to think about the matter of praise.

Corollary III. The pastor can do something to correct this evil. The old system of explaining the Psalm had some merits. It tended to keep the sentiment of the Psalms before the minds of the singers. As a substitute, let the pastor spend a few moments in each service in pointing out the beauty, sweetness, and richness of the portion selected for the praise service. The people can then more easily sing with the spirit and the understanding."

The Singing of God's Word develops Character

"It has been demonstrated in long years of experience that the exclusive use of the Psalms as the matter of praise develops a strong and sturdy and devout type of Christian character. The same cannot be said of the songs of merely human composition. In these days when thee is so much moral weakness and flabbiness of character, when convictions are held so lightly, and moral boundary lines are marked so very indistinctly, there is need that the whole Church get back to the strong old songs of divine inspiration. They will put iron in the blood. They will put strength into the purposes. They will make men humble before God, but mighty for His truth's sake when they stand before men. They will give us for these days character like that of the Covenanters and the Huguenots and the Puritans, men who know God and will dare to be true. And that is the sort of revival which the Church most needs."

–Rev. W. I. Wishart[1]

---

[1] The Psalms in Worship, ibid, page 58.

THE SUITABLENESS AND SUFFICIENCY OF THE PSALTER FOR CHRISTIAN WORSHIP[1]

By President J. A. Thompson, D. D. Tarkio, Mo.

Who questions the suitableness and sufficiency of the Psalter for Christian Worship? The question is found in the sphere of the Church's practice. A large part of the Christian Church has abandoned the use of the Psalter in the praise service; another large part makes small use of it. Dr. Archibald Alexander Hodge was accustomed to tell his classes that the United Presbyterian Church has been raised up in the providence of God to keep the Psalter before the Church. In the fulfillment of its destiny the United Presbyterian Church finds it necessary to champion the suitableness and sufficiency of the Psalter for Christian worship.

What is the formal worship of God? It is outward expression of an inward attitude toward God. It may assume several forms. It is seen in prayer, in praise, in preaching, in the sacraments, in giving, and in fasting. These forms may be divided into two general classes. In all cases the "form" of worship is prescribed in God's Word. No one would think of attempting the formal worship of God in any way not prescribed in His Word. In prayer, in fasting, and in giving the "matter" is not prescribed other than in general terms. We may give to God anything that has value to us. We may fast or any one of a great variety of reasons. We may pray for any one of a multitude of things. "I will therefore that men pray everywhere, lifting up holy hands, without wrath and doubting" (I Tim. ii. 8). "Pray without ceasing. In everything give thanks: for this is the will of God in Christ Jesus concerning you" (I Thess. v. 17, 18). In the sacraments and in praise the "matter" is prescribed to men. No orthodox Christian would think of substituting anything for the bread and wine which the Master used in ordaining His Supper. Whatever disputes Christians may have over the mode of Baptism, they do not dispute over the use of water as its symbol. In preaching we have the combination of the prescribed and the voluntary. It is in part instruction concerning God derived from His Word and in part testimony concerning our own experience of God. Praise belongs to that type of worship based entirely upon what God has revealed of Himself and of man. "Whoso offereth praise glorifieth Me" (Ps. I. 23). God must reveal Himself as a foundation of praise. "O Lord, open Thou my lips; and my mouth shall show forth Thy praise" (Ps. li. 15).

There has been no change in the basic idea of praise. The eternal God remains the same. He is "the Father of lights, with Whom is no

---

[1] The Psalms in Worship, ibid, pages 178-187.

variableness, neither shadow of tuning." Evangelical Christians agree in the belief that the Canon of revelation is closed. God has accomplished His purpose with men in revelation. There is no need for further revelation. The completion of the Canon has been definitely and finally declared. In completing the Canon God did not deem it necessary to add to the book of praise after the period of the Exile. Every feature of worship had been provided for in the Psalter. Christianity did not claim to be a new religion. It was the fruition of the religion of the Old Testament. The Jehovah of Israel's prophets and the Father of our Lord are one and the same. Christianity has no new principle of praise worship to offer. It changed the form of he sacraments to meet new facts in the history of religion. It has given new vitality to prayer and clearer interpretation to praise. It has nothing to add to the character of God, nothing to tell of His relation to men which had not already been uttered by the Holy Ghost through the men whom He had inspired of old.

The Psalter was prepared and inspired for us in the praise service of the Church. No other portion of Scripture has any appearance of having bee prepared for such use. The Psalter assumes this claim. It has not been denied. No one affirms that any other part of the Canon has been prepared for permanent use in the service of song. The title of the Psalter in the Hebrew, as in the Greek, assumes this purpose. "*Sepher Tehilliim*" signifies "a book of praise songs." "*Mizmor*," the title of many individual Psalms, implies a portion prepared for singing. The Psalter is filled with the language of Praise, "Bless Jehovah, O my soul"; "Praise ye Jehovah"; "Oh sing unto Jehovah a new song," are phrases constantly recurring in the Psalms.

Every believer in the inspired Bible accepts the Book of Psalms as a part of the Canon of Scripture. He believes that God is the author of the Psalter. David and Asaph and Moses and Solomon and Ethan and Heman and others penned these Psalms, but the Holy Spirit guided their pens. He is their real Author. When we recall this, and also that there are no other books of praise of which any Christian believes God to be the author, it becomes sacrilegious to call in question the suitableness and sufficiency of the Psalms in Christian worship. We have found that the place of song in worship is to exalt God. In order to exalt Him we must know Him. "Canst thou by searching find out God?" To whom can we turn for a revelation of God sufficient for purposes of worship but to Himself? Praise demands such a knowledge of God that we should feel the need of a divinely inspired book of praise even before its publication. How much folly men have been guilty of in their attempt to supply such a book even after all the revelation of God made in His Word!

The variety of topics dealt with in the Psalter commends it as suitable and sufficient for use in Christian worship. If one has not studied the Psalms topically he will be amazed when he is told of the great number of topics with which they deal. In a very slight analysis, such as is made Nave's Topical Bible, there are thirteen different heads under which the Psalms are classified. The Psalter published by the United Presbyterian Board of Publication, in an analysis confessedly incomplete, finds ninety-two classes of topics dealt with in the Psalter. The Bible Songs, published by the same Board, finds one hundred and fifty-four topics, with important subheads under forty-six of these. The Book of Worship published by the Lutheran Church contains two hundred and sixty-five topics with very few subheads. It might be a question whether such topics as "Conferences and Synods," "Confirmation," "Consecration of Churches," Dedication of Churches," "Election of Pastors or Church Officers," "Marriage," "National Hymns," etc., lie within the sphere of worship proper. An examination of the Psalter shows that it contains material for use in praise God in private devotions or family worship morning and evening, in the Sabbath school, in the prayer meeting, and the church service. I may assume sufficient familiarity with the Psalter on the part of those who read this paper to make it unnecessary to quote in proof of the statements made here with reference to it. It contains praise for the Father, for the Son, and for the Holy Spirit. It contains suitable expression for adoration, confession, petition, praise, and thanksgiving. It has material for use in times of sorrow and of joy, of deepest despondency and of highest hope, of fear and of cheerful confidence, of temptation and of victory over temptation. It encourages the young and vigorous, and comforts the aged and feeble. It gives comfort to those in poverty, and advice to those whom God has blessed with riches. It far outruns the most advanced Christian in its missionary spirit and promise. It sets before Christ's Church the glorious culmination of missions, when "He shall have dominion also from sea to sea, and from the river unto the ends of the earth." It anathematizes sin and glorifies righteousness. It honors the house of God, the day of God, and the Word of God. It anticipates the teaching of the Master with reference to faith, hope, and charity, justice mercy, and righteousness. Its pages sing of the enemies of righteousness and of their destruction. They sing also of the blessedness of the righteous and of their final honor. They magnify the communion of the saints. The Psalter tells of hell and of heaven, of retribution and of reward, of judgment and of mercy. It contains consolation for the sick and dying, prayers for those who are helpless and thanksgiving for recovery from sickness. It is an inspired writer who advises those whom he addresses, "Is any merry? let him sing Psalms." Is there any sphere of song demanded in Christian worship which the Psalter does not supply? I have heard the Psalter criticized by one who had been trained to sing Psalms from childhood because of its supposed insufficiency for the use of children. This was years ago, when the Church had not yet studied the Psalter with a view to its musical possibilities. When this study was begun it was found that there was an abundance of material in the Psalter for the use of children. The criticism of this earnest Christian worker should have been of the music which we once used with the Psalms, not of the Psalms. The Church has supplied the deficiency in some measure. There is still much to be done toward supplying suitable music for use with the Psalter among children. Its versatility adapts the Psalter in a peculiar manner for use in the Sabbath schools. It has somewhat for all classes of Bible students. It certainly saves the Sabbath school of those churches which use it from the reproach which falls so heavily upon the silliness into which uninspired song for children has surely degenerated.

Some critics have objected to the use of the Psalter in Christian worship because it speaks of Christ and of His work only in anticipation, and because it uses the language of Old Testament symbolism when it does deal with the facts and teachings of Christianity. It might be sufficient answer to these critics that the Holy Spirit, the best judge of the suitableness of material for Christian worship, has not seen fit to provide any material for use in the praise service since the coming of Christ in person. That fact will at least suffice to suggest that the Holy Spirit had good reason for completing God's Canon of praise before the Son God became incarnate. May it not have been the purpose of the Holy Spirit to emphasize the "eternal now" in which the Godhead dwells, to keep us of the latter day mindful of the great truth that "in the beginning was the Word, and the Word was with God, and the Word was God," that "the same was in the beginning with God"? May this not be the divine way of teaching the Church that "Jesus Christ is the same yesterday and to-day, yea and forever"? There is a majesty about the conception of Christianity which adapts its worship to the ages of the ages, which permits Abraham and Isaac and Jacob and Moses and Samuel and David and Elijah and John the Baptist and John the Beloved Disciple and James and Peter and Paul and Augustine and Calvin and Knox and all the saints of all time to join in one grand paean of praise, of which the Author is the Master of the musicians Himself.

The Psalter has proved its suitableness and sufficiency for Christian worship in the experience of men. Our Lord set the example for His Church in the service of praise as in everything else. Our Lord made much use of the Psalter in His teaching and preaching, as do Christians of every name. More than seventy distinct references to it are made in the record of His work as given by the Evangelists. Their reports show that no other Book of the Old Testament is referred to as often by our Lord. Only once do we have and direct reference to a praise service in which our Lord took part. In Matt. xxvi. 30, duplicated in Mark xiv. 26, Jesus and His disciples are represented as singing together a portion of the Hallel, Pss. cxiii-cxviii. His use alone of the Psalter should insure its use by His Church through the ages of the ages. The lips of our divine Master not only read, but sang, the words which His Spirit had composed.

In the inspired record of the Apostolic Church there are numerous references to the Praise of God. In Acts ii. 47 the infant Christian Church is mentioned as "praising God and having favor with all the people." The lame man whose story is told in the third chapter of Acts, and who's healing caused so much of excitement among the Jewish dignitaries, is said to have entered the temple "walking and leaping and praising God." Paul and Silas in the inner dungeon of the Philippian prison were "praying and singing hymns unto God" when the earthquake shattered the thick walls of their prison and loosed the chains which bound them. There are references to the service of praise as a familiar part of God's worship in those well-known passages in Ephesians v. 19 and Col. iii. 16. We have no reason whatever to think that any of these passages refer to the use of any other praises than those voiced by God in His own Book. It would be irrational to think of anything else being used or even thought of in formal worship in the temple, the common place of worship during, and following, the Pentecostal period.

The oldest uninspired Christian hymn of which we have any knowledge is that of Clement of Alexandria, composed about 200 A. D., characterized by Dr. Schaff as "a sublime, but somewhat turgid, song of praise to Christ." The use of uninspired hymns did not become general until the close of the fourth century. The uninspired hymn was introduced by those who had peculiar views to exploit. Its spread was quickened by the spread of heresy and by the degeneracy of the Greek and Latin Churches.

A revival of the ancient use of the Psalter came with the Reformation of the sixteenth century. In Germany, in France, in Switzerland, in Scotland, and in Ireland the use of the Psalms was almost universal in the Reformed Churches. It is only fair to add that they did not all use the Psalms exclusively. Savonarola went to the stake in Florence singing the Forty-Sixth Psalm. Luther's dauntless courage at Worms was stimulated by the stirring music of the same glorious Psalm. Huss's martyr soul and the life of the gentle Melancthon went out while the words of God's own songs were upon their lips. The Waldenses in Italy knew no other music during the centuries of their struggle for religious liberty. The Huguenots marched to victory behind the white plume of Henry of Navarre, or sank to death with the noble Coligny on St Bartholomew's Day, singing the Psalms to Marot's music. The words of God's songs were in the mouths of our Scottish ancestors, alike as they signed the covenant with their own warm blood in Greyfriars' Churchyard or sealed the same covenant with martyr blood under the trampling hoofs of the "bluidy Clavers." Let it not be forgotten that the men who withstood the butcher Alva in the cities of Holland, and whose Dutch obstinacy wrung victory from the best efforts of Spain, were men who sang Psalms. The Psalter has taught those who used it to die for Christ's crown and covenant. Under its heroic spell even gentle women have suffered the loss of all things for Christ's sake. Its words have inspired to missionary zeal and missionary courage since the days of the Apostles. It has actually served God's purposes for worship for generations of godly Christians. Today those who stand for the exclusive use of God's inspired Psalter in worship may everywhere be counted upon not only to defend and extend the truth, but take a hand in every genuine effort for reform.

Finally, every attempt to improve upon the Psalter has been compelled to resort to the Psalter for its basic elements. The Church of Jesus Christ to-day knows no canon of praise other than that established by the divine Psalter. In multitudes of cases the very words of uninspired hymns have been suggested by the divine Psalter. The oldest Christian hymn extant, that of Clement of Alexandria, to which reference has already been made, begins "Shepherd of tender youth." Its metaphor is that of the Twenty-Third Psalm. Watts called his best-known and most-used hymnal "The Psalms of David Imitated in the language of the New Testament." "Lead me to the Rock that is higher than I" and its succeeding stanzas, "I will dwell in Thy tabernacle forever, I will take refuge in the covert of Thy wings" (Ps. lxi. 2, 4), are the mighty originals which suggested Toplady's "Rock of Ages, cleft for me." "As the hart panteth after the water brooks, so panteth my soul after Thee, O God" might well have attuned the soul which inspired "Nearer, my God, to Thee, nearer to Thee, nearer to Thee." There is nothing good in the poetry of the uninspired praise which has not been anticipated in God's praise-book, the Psalter. The best thing which can be said of the modern hymnals is the fact that they do so closely imitate the Word of God.

To sum up: the worship of the true God is essentially the same in all ages. Christian worship does not differ in its essential from the worship offered by Abraham.

The Psalter was prepared and compiled for use in the worship of praise. Its author was God. His knowledge of Himself and of man gives Him infinite superiority over any merely human writer of praise.

The Psalter deals with a variety of topics amply sufficient to supply any possible demand that may be made upon it for purposes of worship.

The Psalter has proved its suitableness and sufficiency for Christian worship in the experience of the Church during many centuries and under many conditions.

Every attempt to improve upon the Psalter has been compelled to resort to the Psalter for its basic elements.

I know no surer index of the suitableness and sufficiency of God's own holy words for Christian worship than to ask you to listen to a number of our Lord's own precepts, and then to these same precepts as anticipated and summed up in the most tender verse of the Psalter, the best beloved in the experience of Christ's little ones. Listen! "I am the good Shepherd" (John x. II). "But seek ye first His kingdom, and His righteousness; and all these things shall be added unto you" (Matt. vi. 33). "I am the door; by Me if any man enter in, he shall be saved, and shall go in and out, and find pasture" (John x. 9). "For the Lamb that is in the midst of the throne shall be their shepherd, and shall guide them unto the fountains of waters of life; and God shall wipe away every tear from their eyes" (Rev. vii. 17).

> "The Lord's my shepherd, I'll not want.
> He makes me down to lie
> In pastures green; He leadeth me
> The quiet waters by.
> My soul He doth restore again;
> And me to walk doth make
> Within the paths of righteousness,
> E'en for His own name's sake.
> Yea, though I walk through death's dark vale,
> Yet will I fear no ill,
> For Thou art with me, and Thy rod
> And staff me comfort still.
> A table Thou hast furnished me
> In presence of my foes;
> My head Thou dost with oil anoint,
> And my cup overflows.
> Goodness and mercy all my life
> Shall surely follow me,
> And in God's house for evermore
> My dwelling place shall be."

"The Shepherd Psalm" did not reach the fullness of its meaning until our Lord had said, "I am the good Shepherd."

The World is Not Worthy[1]
Hebrews 11:32-40

"They were stoned, they were sawn asunder, were tempted, were slain with the sword; they wandered about in sheepskins and goatskins; being destitute, afflicted, tormented; (**of whom the world was not worthy**); they wandered in deserts, and in mountains, and in dens and caves of the earth."

–Hebrews 11:37-38 [2]

Introduction

The saints who have gone on before us, would claim with Paul, "For to me to live is Christ, and to die is gain" (Phil. 1:21) Faith sustains the Christian, embracing the Savior, whose grace is sufficient in life and in death. Faith is a wonderful gift from God. Faith embraces our Father in heaven, believing that He loves us with an unconditional and everlasting mercy. Faith embraces our Savior, Christ Jesus the Son of God, believing that His love embraced us in His dying on His cross for our sin and guilt. Faith embraces our Comforter, the Holy Spirit, believing that He walks along the side of us, teaching us the way, and the truth, and the life, even Christ Himself, our King of kings.

The Psalmist's question can be asked today, "Why do the heathen rage, and the people imagine a vain thing?" The answer is also applicable today, "The kings of the earth set themselves, and the rulers take counsel together, against the Lord, and against his anointed, saying, Let us break their bands asunder, and cast away their cords from us." (Ps. 2:1-3). Those who are enemies of God, and desire to take away the Crown-rights of His Anointed King, must heed this warning: "Be wise now therefore, O ye kings; be instructed, ye judges of the earth. Serve the Lord with fear, and rejoice with trembling. Kiss the Son, lest he be angry and ye perish from the way,[3] when his wrath is kindled but a little. Blessed are all they that put their trust in him" (2:10-12).

By Faith They Lived and Died! [Hebrews 11:32-38]

Come with me to the saints who have gone on before — look to them as examples of those whose faith shined before God, of whom He said the world was not worthy. In the sight of God the Father, Son, and

---

[1] Adapted from a sermon delivered by Pastor La May on April 19, 1998 at the Hetherton Reformed Presbyterian Church, Johannesburg, Michigan.

[2] Scripture quotes from the Authorized Version.

[3] Blessed is the man that walketh not in the counsel of the ungodly, nor standeth in the way of sinners, nor sitteth in the seat of the scornful. But his delight is in the law of the Lord; and in his law doth he meditate day and night." –Psalm 1:1-2

Holy Spirit, the world is not worthy to have such a people dwell among them.

There was Gideon, who, with a small army of 300 men, by faith, destroyed the army of the Midianites and Amalekites, "and all the children of the east lay along in the valley like grasshoppers for multitude; and their camels were without number, as the sand by the sea-side for multitude" (Jud. 7:12). There was Samson, who, by faith, could say, "With the jawbone of an ass, heaps upon heaps, with the Jaw of an ass have I slain a thousand men" (Jud. 15:16). There was the day when the Lord "discomfited Sisera, and all his chariots, and all his host, with the edge of the sword before Barak; so that Sisera lighted down off his chariot, and fled away on his feet" (Jud. 4:15).

The Lord's servants, through faith, subdued kingdoms, wrought righteousness, obtained promises, and stopped the mouths of lions. Daniel was delivered from the den of lions, testifying, "My God hath sent his angel, and hath shut the lions' mouths, that they have not hurt me; forasmuch as before him innocency was found in me; and also before thee, O king, have I done no hurt" (Dan. 6:22). God's saints quenched the violence of fire, escaped the edge of the sword, and out of weakness were made strong, and were valiant in battle.

The saints of the Lord "had trial of cruel mockings and scourgings, yea, moreover of bonds and imprisonment; they were stoned, they were sawn asunder, were tempted, were slain with the sword" (Heb. 11:36-37). "Precious in the sight of the Lord is the death of his saints. O Lord, truly I am thy servant" (Ps. 116:15-16). One of those saints could witness to this truth, His servant, Stephen. With a gnashing of their teeth, Christ's enemies threw their stones. However, Stephen, filled with the Holy Spirit, "looked up steadfastly into heaven, and saw the glory of God, and Jesus standing at the right hand of God, and said, Behold, I see the heavens opened, and the Son of man standing at the right hand of God" (Acts 7:55-56).

These saints belonged to those *"of whom the world was not worthy."* However, "They shall behold the glorified body of Jesus Christ; and if it be pleasant to behold the sun, how blessed a sight will it be to see Christ, the Sun of Righteousness, clothed with our human nature, shining in glory above the angels." (Thomas Watson, <u>A Body of Divinity</u>).

Saints of Royalty

Not only out of every tribe, tongue, and nation, does God draw His saints, but from the very courts of kings. For the Worthy of the Lord are those who stand firm in the faith delivered to them by Christ, no matter where and when they stand. How mightily the Lord works in the kingdoms of this world. There is King Edward VI[1], who was the son of that infamous king Henry VIII. His mother was Jane Seymour, who died twelve days after he was born.

King Henry VIII cared much for the welfare of his children. And by our Lord's providential care for His people, King Henry was used to place his son, Edward, under learned and pious teachers. Under such teachers Edward grew to learn both his languages and the Word of God. Curio, the Italian Reformer, speaking of the tutors, Cheke and Cook, said, "That by their united prayers, counsels, and industry, they had formed a king of the highest, even divine hopes." This hope was seen to come true when, at the age of 10, his father king Henry VIII died on January 28, 1547. The prayer of this new young king embraced these words, "I am the price of thy son's death, Jesus Christ; for thy Son's sake thou wilt not lose me. . . . For this cause, Lord God, I am bold to speak to thy Majesty. Thou Lord, by thy providence hast called me to rule; make me able to follow thy calling. Thou, Lord, by thine order hast committed an anointed king to my governance; direct me therefore with thy hand, that I err not from thy good pleasure."

His coronation took place on February 28. The address of Archbishop Cranmer to this youthful king was embraced by Edward throughout his short reign. In part Cranmer charged Edward, saying, "Your majesty is God's vice-regent, and Christ's vicar within your own dominions, and to see, with your predecessor Josiah, God truly worshiped, and idolatry destroyed; the tyranny of the bishops of Rome banished from your subjects, and images removed. . . . You are to reward virtue, to revenge sin, to justify the innocent, to relive the poor, to procure peace, to repress violence, and to execute justice throughout your realms."

Three swords were brought in at his coronation, "emblematical of his three kingdoms. Edward said that there was still one sword wanting. Asked what it would be, Edward answered, "The Bible!" He continued, "That book is the sword of the Spirit, and to be preferred before these swords. That aught in all right to govern us, who use them for the people's safety by God's appointment. Without the sword we are nothing, we can do nothing, we have no power. . . . He that rules without it, is not to be called God's minister, or a king. Under that we ought to live, to fight, to govern the people, and to perform all our affairs. From that alone we obtain all power, virtue, grace, salvation, and whatsoever we have of divine strength."

---

[1] The Lives of the British Reformers, Presbyterian Board of Publication, Philadelphia.

The premature death of King Edward VI of England brought an alarming change to his court. Both church and state would soon feel, again, the arm of persecution. Young King Edward was sick for a long time, during which he made a will, bequeathing the English crown to Lady Jane, the daughter of the duke of Suffolk. She was married to Lord Guildford. By this will he hoped to supersede the succession of Mary and Elizabeth, his two sisters, to the throne. There was great anxiety about the return of Roman Catholicism to the nation.

Lady Jane was of the same age of King Edward.[1] Born in 1537, she was of royal blood, her mother's mother was daughter to Henry VII, her grandmother on her father's side, was queen consort to Edward IV. She had a beautiful hand with the needle and writing, along with the ability to write and speak in French, Italian, Latin, and Greek. She was a woman of the Reformation, being versed in the truths thereof. With the intercession of her mother, and the persuasions of Northumberland, Lady Jane somberly assented. With a heavy heart she was brought, by water, to the Tower. About six in the afternoon she was proclaimed queen, reigning for only a period of fourteen days.

Mary was proclaimed queen, under false promises, which took place at Westminster, becoming a signal for the bloody persecution which followed. Separated from her husband, Lady Jane was placed in confinement, imprisoned in the Tower along with members of her family and nobility. She and her husband, along with Cranmer and others, were arraigned for high treason. They pleaded guilty. Her guilt rested in her faith. Our Lord was faithful even more. For we note that Judge Morgan, who pronounced the sentence of death upon her, became raving mad, "in which state he died, incessantly calling out that the lady Jane should be taken from his sight."

Lady Jane's husband was killed before her. She could only wave to him as they took him away. And upon hearing the cart returning, she beheld his body, saying, "O Guildford, Guildford, the anterepast is not so bitter that you have tasted, and that I shall soon taste, as to make my flesh tremble; it is nothing compared to the feast that you and I shall this day partake of in heaven." After about an hour, Lady Jane was led to the scaffold. From the scaffold she witnessed to her faith, saying, "I pray you all, good Christian people, to bear me witness that I die a good Christian woman, and that I do look to be saved by no other means, but only by the mercy of God in the blood of his only Son Jesus Christ." Lady Jane also witnessed to her need for repentance, saying, "and I do

---

[1] The Lives of the British Reformers, ibid. See also Fox's Book of Martyrs Zondervan Pub. House; and a delightful novel by Deborah Meroff, Coronation of Glory, Zondervan Pub. House.

now confess, that when I did know the word of God, I neglected the same, and loved myself and the world." She did not lay the blame upon her killers but upon herself as a sinner, yet knowing the forgiveness of her Savior. Asking for the prayers of the saints, and then seeing the executioner kneel before her, asking her forgiveness, "whom she forgave most willingly," she kneeled down, tied the handkerchief about her own eyes, commending herself to the Lord, she died, February 12, 1554.

Where are those who exemplify such lives as those of young Edward and Lady Jane? Are we worthy of the name of our Lord and Savior Jesus Christ, in what we do, in what we say, and in the place where we are? Are we about the Lord's business in the bringing up of our children in the name of our Lord, being taught, and teaching the doctrines which God Himself has given us in His Word, Written. Let us not forget those who have gone on before, giving of their blood, that the Gospel of Christ and His blood may be unashamedly displayed and proclaimed. As they were faithful unto death, "Lord Jesus, let us not fail Thee."

By Faith The Saints Continue to Live & Die. [Hebrews 11:38-40]

The saints, of whom the world is not worthy, are still persecuted, imprisoned, and killed. However, in whatever way the Children of God die, they do not die in vain. Those who have gone on before are examples for us. We have been given the same gift of faith. This faith, in Christ, sustains us in all kinds of situations, sicknesses, persecutions, and physical death. Blessed are His people, for they die in the Lord! God looks upon His people in covenant love, declaring that the world is not worthy of such a people.

From their homes and churches, from the halls of congress and parliaments, from dungeons of persecution, and scaffolds of death, the people of God must stand firm in faith in Christ and His glorious Word. We are followers and witnesses of the Christ and His Gospel. We are those who rest upon the love of God and the power of the Holy Spirit. We are not of the world, but in it as pilgrims. John Calvin insists, "So also ought we be animated so as boldly to despise the world; and were it to cast us out, let us know that we go forth from a fatal gulf, and that God thus provides for our safety, so that we may not sink in the same destruction" (Calvin's Commentary).

Those, who by faith, of whom the world is not worthy, roam the deserts and the mountains, all of whom, "having obtained a report through faith, received not the promise; God having provided some better thing for us, that they without us should not be made perfect" (Heb. 11:39-40).

God has provided something better for us. And we will, before our

Father in heaven, on a new heaven and new earth, receive the better promise, along with all of God's saints, God's people. We live each day with this promise. We seek the maturity that only a child of God can receive in Christ. We desire the righteous and moral life, according to the Law of God our King, because we look forward to His promise. We live in love because the God, who has loved us, loves us with an everlasting love. We study His Word that we might be strong in the faith that when trials and testings come we can testify to His promises. Our daily lives become a measure of our faith in Christ, the living King of kings!

Our prayers, our Bible studies, our worship and service, our fellowship with one another, and our praise and witness, become as spies sent into the Promise Land. The fruit thereof gives us a taste of that eternal glory, speaking to us as did Joshua and Caleb when they returned from searching the land of Canaan, saying, "We came unto the land whither thou sentest us, and surely it floweth with milk and honey; and this is the fruit of it" (Num. 13:27). As Thomas Watson writes of the Christian: "A true saint every day takes a turn in heaven; his thoughts and desires are, like cherubims, flying up to paradise, Can men of the world delight in contemplating their glory in reversion? Could we send forth faith as a spy, and everyday view the glory of the Jerusalem above, how would it rejoice us, as it does the heir to think of the inheritance which is to come into his hand shortly?"

God's Conclusion

The Sovereign Lord has the last word — or laugh — as He has set His Son as King over all nations. "Sit Thou at My right hand, until I make Thine enemies Thy footstool" (Ps. 110:1; Matt. 22:44). "He that sitteth in the heavens shall laugh; the Lord shall have them in derision. Then shall he speak unto them in his wrath, and vex them in his sore displeasure. Yet have I set my king upon my holy hill of Zion" (Ps. 2:4-6). The beloved apostle John heard a voice of a great multitude, "as the voice of many waters, and as the voice of mighty thunderings, saying, Alleluia; for the Lord God omnipotent reigneth. Let us be glad and rejoice, and give honor to him; for the marriage of the Lamb is come, and his wife hath made herself ready" (Rev. 19:6-7).

For Christ's Crown and Covenant[1]
OUR BANNER BLUE

Our royal ensign waves in sight;
Banner Blue, our Banner Blue!
Here Scotland's manhood served with might;
Banner Blue, our Banner Blue!
Our Country's flag we never slight;
In its defense we serve and fight,
Yet ever true to Christ and right;
Banner Blue, our Banner Blue!

Our father's blood 'neath it was shed;
Banner Blue, our Banner Blue!
On many fields these martyrs bled;
Banner Blue, our Banner Blue!
The truth it bears is crimson red,
Yet we advance with lifted head,
We march with no uncertain tread;
Banner Blue, our Banner Blue!

The precious dust of Scotland's slain,
Banner Blue, our Banner Blue!
Shall not be sacrificed in vain;
Banner Blue, our Banner Blue!
The truth forever is the same;
Christ's Kingship we shall still proclaim,
Till all the world adores His name;
Banner Blue, our Banner Blue!

The torch of truth from Scotia's hand,
Banner Blue, our Banner Blue!
Falls at our feet's burning brand;
Banner Blue, our Banner Blue!
We catch it up at His command,
It's flame will light up every land;
Christ's Crown and Cov'nant firm shall stand;
Banner Blue, our Banner Blue!
-Rev. D. H. Elliott, D.D.-

---

[1] The Blue Banner was first carried by the Covenanters when they withstood the attack of King Charles I at Dunse Law in 1639; an ensign declaring Christ as King of kings and Lord of lords.

THE BANNER OF THE COVENANT

On special occasions in both the Old and New Testaments, believers covenanted together that they would obey the Lord. At the time of the Reformation, believers in Scotland adopted this practice for mutual protection and for the advancement of Biblical Christianity. On at least three occasions -- 1581, 1638, and 1643 -- the entire nation covenanted in this way.

These covenants embraced the whole orb of Christian faith and experience, emphasizing such great themes as repentance, grace, and obedience. They also maintained that the King (or the state) cannot govern the church, and that the State itself must recognize the supreme Kingship of Christ. The Reformed believers, known as Covenanters (from their support of the covenants), insisted on "the crown rights of King Jesus", which brought them into conflict with those who supported "the divine right of kings."

 The blue banner bearing the motto "For Christ's Crown and Covenant" originated as a battle flag for these Covenanters. It first appeared in 1639 with the Covenanter army under General Alexander Leslie, First Earl of Leven. During the period of most intense persecution (1660-1668), some 18,000 men, women, and children died in battle, were executed, killed without process of law, or exiled, for their faithfulness to "Christ's Crown and Covenant".

Since the end of the "killing time", the Blue Banner has continued to serve as a symbol of the Reformed Faith. The Reformed Presbyterian Church is the continuation of the Covenanter church in Scotland, and treasures the testimony and heritage which God has given it. The banner serves as a reminder of our commitment to the great truths of the Word of God.

-Author Unknown

BATTLE HYMN OF THE CHRISTIAN CHURCH
Words: Dr. Francis Nigel Lee.[1]
Music: "John Brown's Body"

My eyes have seen the glory of Jehovah our great King
For our God is trampling Satan. Hallelu-Jah! Let us sing!
With His Word, we'll hammer humanists; to Jesus, converts bring
For Christ goes reigning on!

Glory, glory, hallelu-Jah
Sing the psalms to our Lord Jesus!
Sing the psalms to our Lord Jesus!
For Christ goes reigning on!

I have seen Him in the pulpits of His Christocratic Church.
He is making us His soldiers, while His Word we gladly search!
As we fight His righteous battles, He'll not leave us in the lurch.
For Christ goes reigning on!

When He rose, He blew the trumpet that shall never sound defeat!
He is sifting out the hearts of men, before His judgment seat.
Let me, too, help crush His enemies! Subdue them, O my feet!
For Christ goes reigning on!

We will serve Jehovah-Jesus, in the storms and in the calms.
We will gladly sing out loud, all the imprecatory psalms.
We'll impose God's Law against all thugs, with never any qualms.
For Christ goes reigning on!

In the beauty of the New Earth, there'll be neither sin nor sea.
For the Lord's bride will be happy, in her blissful "slavery" --
While the wicked burn eternally in hell, from virtue "free"
For Christ goes reigning on!

---

[1] The Works of Rev. Prof. Dr. F.N. Lee, web site: dr-fnlee.org

Epitaph:

These all died in faith.[1] — Hebrews 11:13

BEHOLD THE EPITAPH of all those blessed saints who fell asleep before the coming of our Lord! It matters nothing how else they died, whether of old age, or by violent means; this one point, in which they all agree, is the most worthy of record, *"they all died in faith."* In faith they lived; it was their comfort, their guide, their motive and their support. And in the same spiritual grace they died, ending their life-song in the sweet strain in which they had so long continued. They did not die resting in the flesh or upon their own attainments; they made no advance from their first way of acceptance with God, but held to the way of faith to the end. Faith is as precious to die by as to live by.

Dying in faith has distinct reference to the past. They believed the promises which had gone before, and were assured that their sins were blotted out through the mercy of God. Dying in faith has to do with the present. These saints were confident of their acceptance with God; they enjoyed the beams of His love, and rested in His faithfulness. Dying in faith looks into the future. They fell asleep, affirming that the Messiah would surely come, and that when He should in the last days appear upon the earth, they would rise from their graves to behold Him. To them the pains of death were but the birth-pangs of a better state.

Take courage, my soul, as you read this epitaph. Your course, through grace, is one of faith, and sight seldom cheers you. This has also been the pathway of the brightest and the best. Faith was the orbit in which these stars of the first magnitude moved all the time of their shining here; and happy are you that it is yours. Look anew tonight to Jesus, *"the author and finisher of your faith,"* and thank Him for giving you like precious faith with souls now in glory.

–Charles Spurgeon

"These all died in faith, not having received the promises, but having seen afar off, and were persuaded of them, and embraced them, and confessed that they were strangers and pilgrims on the earth."
–Hebrews 11:13

---

[1] C. H. Spurgeon, <u>Morning and Evening</u>, The Devotional Classics, Sovereign Grace Trust Fund, LaFayette, In., 1990, May 2nd, Evening.

Bibliography

Alexander, J. A., The Acts of the Apostles, The Banner of Truth Trust, Edinburgh, 1984.

Anderson, James, The Ladies of The Covenant, Blackie & Son, Glasgow, 1850.

Baxter, Richard, The Saints' Everlasting Rest, The National Foundation for Christian Education, Marshallton, Delaware.

Bible, The Geneva Bible, 1599, L. L. Brown Publishing, 1990.

Bible, Key Word Study Bible, King James Version, AMG Publishers, Chattanooga, TN, 1991.

Boettner, Loraine, Studies in Theology, The Presbyterian and Reformed Publishing, Co., January 1985.

Boettner, Loraine, The Reformed Doctrine of Predestination, The Presbyterian and Reformed Publishing Co., Phillipsburg, N. J., 1979.

Budgen, Victor, On Fire For God, Evangelical Press, Hertfordshire, England, 1983.

Bunyan, John, The Pilgrim's Progress, With a life of the Author, and explanatory notes by Rev. W. Mason, William Collins, Sons, & Co., Glasgow.

Calvin, John, Institutes of the Christian Religion, John T. McNeill, ed., two volumes, The Westminster Press, Philadelphia, Pa., 1973

Chilton, David, The Days of Vengeance, Dominion Press, Horn Lake, MS

Christian Martyrs, American Sunday School Union, Philadelphia, Pa.[1]

Covenanter, The, January to December, 1858, C. Aitchison, Belfast.

Complete Works of John Bunyan, The, Bradley, Garretson & Co., Philadelphia, 1874

Dickson, David, The Psalms, The Banner of Truth Trust, Carlisle, Pa., 1995.

Fox's Book of Martyrs, W. B, Forbush, ed., Zondervan Publishing House, Grand Rapids, MI, 1970.

Accounts of Revival, compiled by The Rev. John Gillies, The Banner of Truth Trust, 1981.

Howie, John, The Scots Worthies, Oliphant, Anderson, & Ferrier, Edinburgh.

Knox, John, The Reformation in Scotland, The Banner of Truth Trust, Edinburgh, 1982.

Lives of the British Reformers, The, Presbyterian Board of Publication, Philadelphia.

Macleod, John, Scottish Theology, The Banner of Truth Trust, Edinburgh, 1943.

---

[1] Interesting note in this book: Eastern District of Pennsylvania, to wit: Be it Remembered, that on the twenty seventh day of August, in the fifty-third year of the Independence of the United States of America, A. D. 1828, Paul Beck, Junior, Treasurer in trust for the American Sunday School Union, of the said District, has deposited in this office the title of a book, the right whereof he claims as proprietor, in the words following, to wit:–"Christian Martyrs, or Familiar Conversations on the Sufferings of some Eminent Christians. By the author of "Scenes in Georgia," &c. Written for the American Sunday School Union. "Godlike men, how firm they stood, Seeding their country with their blood."

M'Crie, Thomas The Story of the Scottish Church, Bell and Bain Ltd, Glasgow.

Meroff, Deborah, Coronation of Glory, The story of Lady Jane Grey, Inheritance Publications, Alberta, Canada, 1998.

Murray, John, The Covenant of Grace, Presbyterian and Reformed Publishing Co., Phillipsburg, N.J., 1988.

Murray, John J, John Marshall Life and Writings, The Banner of Truth Trust, Carlisle, PA, 2005.

Knox, John, The Reformation in Scotland, The Banner of Truth Trust, Edinburgh, 1982.

Letis, Theodore P., The Ecclesiastical Text, The Institute for Renaissance and Reformation Biblical Studies, Philadelphia, 1997.

Pollok, Robert, Helen of the Glen; A tale of The Scotch Covenanters, Robert Carter, New York, 1841.

Psalms in Worship, The, John McNaugher, Ed, The United Presbyterian Board of Education, Pittsburgh, Pa., 1907.

Psalter, The, A revised edition of the Scottish Metrical Version of the Psalms, Blackie & Son, Dublin, 1881

Psalter, The Book of Psalms for Singing, The Board of Education, RPCNA, Pittsburgh, Pa., 1991.

Psalter, The Comprehensive Psalter, Scottish Metrical Version with Music, Blue Banner Books, A Ministry of First Presbyterian Church, Rowlett, Texas, 2000.

Purves, Jock, Fair Sunshine, The Banner of Truth Trust, Edinburgh, 1990.

Reformed Confessions Harmonized, Joel R. Beeke and Sinclair B. Ferguson, Ed, Baker Books, Grand Rapids, MI.

Rutherford, Samuel, Communion Sermons, Charles Glass & Co., Glasgow, Reprint, James A. Dickson, Edinburgh, 1986.

Rutherford, Samuel, Lex Rex, The Law and The Prince, Sprinkle Publications, Harrisonburg, VA, 1982.

Simpson, Rev. Robert, Traditions of the Covenanters, Presbyterian Board of Publication, Philadelphia.

Spurgeon, C. H., The Treasury of David, in three volumes, MacDonald Publishing Co., McLean, VA.

Spurgeon, C. H., Morning and Evening. Sovereign Grace Trust Fund, Lafayette, Indiana, 1990.

Symington, William, Historical Sketch of The Westminster Assembly of Divines, Presbyterian's Armoury Publications, Australia, 2002.

Symington, William, Messiah the Prince, The Christian Statesman Press, Pittsburgh, Pa., 1999.

Valley of Vision, The, Arthur Bennett, ed., The Banner of Truth Trust, Edinburgh, 1977.

Van Der Jagt, The Escape, *The Adventures of Three Huguenot Children fleeing Persecution based on historical facts*, Inheritance Pub., Alberta, Canada, 1988.

Watson, Thomas, A Body of Divinity, The Banner of Truth Trust, London, 1972.

Watson, Thomas, <u>The Lord's Prayer</u>, The Banner of Truth Trust, London, 1972.

Webster, Noah, <u>American Dictionary of The English Language 1828</u>, Foundation for American Christian Education, 2002.

Westminster Confession of Faith, Free Presbyterian Publications, Glasgow, 2001.